'I honestly didn't know there were so many ways to
toast cheese – genius!'
Patricia Michelson, La Fromagerie

'A collection of unusual and tempting recipes'
Sunday Post

'[*British Cheese on Toast*] reveals how you can upgrade
the simple dish with more than 100 amazing and delicious
recipes ... Steve Parker delves into the UK's top dairy
delights to create delicious flavour combinations.'
Daily Star

'Steve Parker takes you on a tasting tour of British cheeses.'
Take A Break

'Steve Parker recently wrote a book called *British Cheese
on Toast*. Any prime minister would be well advised to
retain him as a special adviser on the subject ...'
The Times

'With a handy guide to shops where artisan cheeses
featured in the book can be bought, as well as tips on
using supermarket, *British Cheese on Toast* is a complete
celebration of this traditional meal. The perfect gift
for cheese lovers everywhere.'
Daily Press

After leaving corporate life, Steve Parker opened an award-winning cheese shop, delicatessen and wine bar in South West London. He has judged national and international food and drink competitions, including the World Cheese Awards, the British Cheese Awards and the Independent Wine Merchant Awards, and has featured in industry publications including *Speciality Food Magazine*, *Wine Merchant*, *Decanter* and *Off Licence News*. He now organises corporate and private food and drink tasting events and is a professional speaker on his favourite subjects of cheese and wine. This is his first book.

BRITISH
CHEESE ON
TOAST

Over 100 recipes
with Farmhouse Cheeses

STEVE PARKER

First published in 2020 by HEADLINE HOME
An imprint of HEADLINE PUBLISHING GROUP

First published in paperback in 2022 by HEADLINE HOME
An imprint of HEADLINE PUBLISHING GROUP

Originally published in Great Britain in 2019 by Steve Parker

2

Cataloguing in Publication Data is available from the British Library

ISBN 978 1 4722 7838 8
eISBN 978 1 4722 7837 1

Commissioning Editor: Lindsey Evans
Senior Editor: Kate Miles
Copy Editor: Anne Sheasby
Proofreader: Margaret Gilbey
Indexer: Caroline Wilding

Designed and typeset by EM&EN
Printed and bound in Great Britain by Clays Ltd, Elcograf S.p.A.

MIX
Paper from
responsible sources
FSC® C104740
www.fsc.org

HEADLINE PUBLISHING GROUP
An Hachette UK Company
Carmelite House
50 Victoria Embankment
London
EC4Y 0DZ

www.headline.co.uk
www.hachette.co.uk

To my Dad, Alan

Contents

INTRODUCTION

There is no doubt that cheese on toast is considered an all-time classic dish loved by generations of people of all ages. It can be enjoyed as a meal or snack at any time of the day, be it breakfast, brunch, lunch, dinner or as a late-night supper. The combination of two fermented products makes for a great pairing and if you add a third fermented product, wine, you create a light meal that is enjoyed in many countries throughout the world.

In Britain, it's usually referred to simply as Cheese on Toast but different combinations of one or two slices of bread can also be called Grilled Cheese, Cheese Toasty, Toasted Cheese, Roasted Cheese or even Choast. The idea is to place cheese on top of a slice of toast and grill it – possibly the quickest and simplest recipe ever!

In 2010, I opened a cheese and wine shop and restaurant which went on to win various food and drink awards, as a result of which I was invited to judge in several major cheese competitions, including the World Cheese Awards. The menu comprised a range of dishes all centred on cheese, including fondue, raclette, tartiflette, cheese boards and other dishes I created myself. Cheese and Bacon Bread and Butter Pudding, anyone?

Without a doubt, the most popular item on the menu was 'Amazing Cheese on Toast' which sold much more than any other item. Simple to make, tasty to eat and popular with everyone. Hardly a day passed without someone asking for the recipe, so after closing the restaurant and shop, after many happy years, to focus on running tasting events and writing, I decided to put pen to paper for the benefit of my former customers.

Why stop at 'Amazing Cheese on Toast'? I thought. Over the years I had created a number of tasty cheese on toast combinations and therefore decided to write a whole book of my recipes.

Despite there being a multitude of great cheeses made around the world, I still maintain that Britain makes the finest range and variety of artisan and farmhouse cheeses, so I decided to make this book about British cheeses only. As I started writing the recipes, the list grew longer and I set myself the target of creating one hundred recipes, all using traditional, artisan or farmhouse cheeses.

This book, containing over one hundred different recipes, builds upon the simple premise of placing cheese on a piece of toast, by using a wide and diverse range of different cheeses, different breads and different accompaniments – all designed to give tasty flavour combinations.

Like so many traditional food combinations, there are an infinite number of personal views on the right and wrong way to make cheese on toast, dependent on geography, local cheeses, family tradition and personal taste.

For the purposes of this book, I have followed a few basic principles. You may agree or disagree but at least you know what 'rules' have been applied.

No Butter: as delicious as melting butter spread on toast is, the combination of two dairy products does not work in my opinion and so the cheese wins and the butter is left in the fridge, except for use in preparing toppings.

No Beans: one of the great meals of all time, much-loved by university students, is beans on toast with grated cheese on top, but it is not cheese on toast and therefore doesn't feature in these pages.

Hot and Cold: many cheese styles lend themselves to being melted but some are better enjoyed as they are, so I have included a few recipes where the cheese is not heated in any way, making them ideal summer dishes.

Supermarket Swaps: each recipe in this book recommends the use of a traditionally made artisan cheese, and also includes a list of some suitable alternative cheeses at the end of the recipe. If, however, you are unable to source a particular artisan cheese, please feel free to use an alternative cheese of your choice. Every British supermarket has a range of cheeses that are made especially for them, some of which are traditionally made and others that are commercially made. It is not the intention of this book to compare or make judgements on these different cheeses in any way, and some of them are truly excellent. Therefore, if you prefer to use a supermarket own-brand cheese or a branded cheese, such as Cathedral City, Pilgrim's Choice or Seriously Strong, then please do so instead.

Perfect Cheese on Toast?

Somewhat unbelievably, in 2013, The British Cheese Board and The Royal Society of Chemistry carried out a scientific study to establish the formula for the perfect cheese on toast. I thought you may be interested to see the results of their research, as follows . . .

$$[(50g \times shC) + (10mm^* \times wB)] \xrightarrow[d-18cm \quad t-4\,mins]{T-115°C^{**}} \text{Perfect cheese on toast}$$

s – sliced   h – hard   C – cheese   w – white   B – bread

T – grill temperature   d – distance from grill   t – time under grill

* – bread thickness (medium sliced)   ** – equivalent to grill on medium heat

For the non-scientific readers, this means you take 50g of sliced hard cheese and place it on top of 10mm-thick toasted white bread. You then put this under a medium grill for 4 minutes at a temperature of 115°C, at a distance of 18cm from the grill.

The researchers evaluated the effect that distance, time and cheese format had on the final result. They found early on that the cheese melted more consistently when the heat source was further away. After zeroing in on the distance, the time was assessed. It had to be just the right time to melt the cheese without burning the edges of the toast. Finally, these highly trained scientists investigated grated, sliced and cubed cheese with sliced cheese being the clear winner.

Further tests established that a hard cheese like Cheddar worked best, and white bread provided the most consistent platform for cheese melting. Clearly this is all a bit silly, but science isn't always a serious business. It is highly simplified, but at least you know how to make scientifically perfect cheese on toast!

The Maillard Reaction

The Maillard reaction refers to a chain of reactions between amino acids and reducing sugars and it is named after the

French chemist Louis-Camille Maillard who first investigated these reactions in 1912.

When a slice of bread is placed into a toaster or under a hot grill, the heating elements rise to an optimum temperature of 154°C, at which point the system is provided with enough thermal energy to begin the Maillard reaction. The reactive carbonyl group of a reducing sugar reacts with the amino group of an amino acid within the bread to produce a nitrogen-substituted glycosylamine molecule. The glycosylamine molecule then isomerises to produce a ketosamine, which undergoes further reactions depending on the environment.

The slightly acidic conditions of white bread (which typically has a pH of 5.0–6.2) allow for the formation of melanoidins, which are long, polymeric pigments (much like the melanin in our skin). And that, dear reader, is why toast turns brown.

Why Does Cheese Melt?

Two things happen. First, at about 32°C, the solid milk fat in the cheese begins to liquefy, the cheese softens, and beads of melted fat rise to the surface. As the cheese gets hotter, the bonds holding together the casein proteins (the principal proteins in cheese) break, and the cheese collapses into a thick fluid. This complete melting occurs at about 54°C for soft, high-moisture cheeses like mozzarella, around 65°C for aged, low-moisture cheeses like Cheddar, and 82°C for hard, dry cheeses like Parmigiano-Reggiano.

Less of the science, let's take a look at the various styles of cheese and bread used in this book, based on taste, flavour and great pairings, not formulas!

It's all About the Cheese

Britain makes over seven hundred different varieties of cheese, covering every conceivable style, restricted only by the availability of milk from indigenous animals. As far as I know, there is no camel's, yak's or donkey's milk cheese produced in Britain despite their widespread use in other parts of the world. In the interests of clarity, for the purposes of this book, all of the cheeses featured are made in either England, Scotland, Wales or Northern Ireland. All the cheeses mentioned here are traditionally made cheeses, most of which are artisan, farmhouse cheeses made using milk from the cheesemakers' own herds of cows, sheep, goats or buffalo. No industrial factory-made cheeses are used. Although the majority of British cheeses are made from cow's milk, there are also a large number of goat's, sheep's and to a lesser extent, buffalo's milk cheeses, which can be within any of the categories listed below.

Fresh Cheeses

❖ Mild cheeses which are ready to eat as soon as they are made and usually eaten within a few weeks. The short maturing time means the full flavours of the milk are predominant, they are nearly always pure white and the texture is always soft and creamy, with no time for any rind to form.

❖ This category includes cow's milk cheeses, which are

typically grassy and slightly sweet, goat's milk cheeses with a slight winey, nutty flavour, and the caramelised flavours of sheep's milk cheeses. Soft buffalo's milk cheeses are also in this category.

❖ Some fresh cheeses are coated in either ash (mainly goat's cheeses) or have been aged for a short time to allow the development of soft rinds.

❖ British examples include British Mozzarella, Fettle, Golden Cross and Ragstone.

Soft, White Cheeses

❖ Soft, creamy cheeses which have developed a brilliant white, soft, velvety rind. The interior usually starts as a firm, chalky, dry texture but during maturation, becomes soft, oozy and runny. They are not pressed and therefore retain a relatively high level of whey and accordingly have a lower percentage of fat.

❖ Flavours start as fresh and grassy, but develop into a mushroom-like aroma and taste as they ripen.

❖ British examples include Tunworth, Bath Soft, Perl Wen and Waterloo.

Semi-Hard Cheeses

❖ As the name suggests, semi-hard cheeses are aged for longer than soft cheeses but not as long as firm or hard cheeses. They have a high moisture content and tend to be milder tasting than other cheeses, with earthy, milky, sweet and tangy flavours.

❖ Usually off-white to pale creamy yellow in colour, the interior is usually smooth and supple, meaning that they are easier to slice without crumbling or breaking.

❖ They can be made with cow's, goat's or sheep's milk.

❖ British examples include Cornish Yarg, Dirty Vicar and Caerphilly.

Washed-Rind Cheeses

❖ Soft or semi-soft cheeses with a soft, thin rind which have been washed in brine or alcohol resulting in a pungent, fruity flavour and a sticky pink or orange rind.

❖ They are nearly always made from cow's milk but a few examples exist using goat's or sheep's milk. Washed-rind cheeses often start with a grainy texture and slowly soften as they ripen, starting under the rind and working to the centre.

❖ British examples include Stinking Bishop, Maida Vale and Rollright.

Firm Cheeses

❖ Pressed cheeses, with either cooked or uncooked curd and a firm but moist texture. By pressing the cheeses, excess whey is eliminated resulting in a firm, smooth texture which maintains its structure when cut.

- Alpine-style cheeses, many of which have naturally formed holes or eyes, are generally firm in texture and therefore are categorised as firm cheeses.

- Firm cheeses are usually matured for at least three months and often years, during which time aromas and flavours develop, until they are strong and tangy.

- Many traditional British cheeses are included in this category, including Lancashire, Wensleydale and Cheshire, which are also referred to as 'crumbly' cheeses.

- British examples include Cheddar, Red Leicester, Rachel and Ogleshield.

Hard Cheeses

- Fully matured cheeses with a brittle, crumbly texture and salty flavour.

- Usually made by cooking the curd and pressing to give a lower moisture content.

- Generally these very hard cheeses are made from cow's or sheep's milk.

- The longer period of maturing results in full flavour cheeses with a distinctive tanginess.

- British examples include Old Winchester, Berkswell, Teifi and Sussex Charmer.

Blue Cheeses

❖ Inoculated with a mould (most commonly *Penicillium roqueforti*) that creates blue veins and develops a tangy, salty flavour.

❖ The blue, green or grey veins develop when the cheese is 'spiked' to allow oxygen to enter the cheese and encourage the growth of the *Penicillium* mould.

❖ They range from soft, creamy and mildly tangy cheeses to full-flavoured, salty styles.

❖ British examples include Stilton, Stichelton, Barkham Blue and Cornish Blue.

Flavoured Cheeses

❖ Additional flavours are either added to the curd before moulding or rubbed into the outside before the rind fully forms. This category includes smoked cheeses, leaf-wrapped or rind-rubbed cheeses, and cheeses with added fruit, herbs or spices.

❖ British examples include Wild Garlic Yarg, Tornegus and Hereford Hop.

Cow's, Goat's, Sheep's and Buffalo's Milk Cheeses

❖ Cow's milk is the most popular milk used for cheesemaking in Britain, but cheese can be made from the milk of most mammals.

- Cows require flat or gently sloping pastures on which to graze, so in areas that have different terrains, such as steep hills or rocky areas, goats or sheep are better suited due to their climbing abilities. They need less grazing pasture, due to being smaller animals, and therefore have proved easier to keep on small farms. The smaller size means that they produce less milk and as a result the cheeses have historically been much smaller than some of their larger cow's milk counterparts.

- Goat's milk contains a higher proportion of fatty acids than cow's milk and it is this that leads to its distinctive tangy flavour, and the lower level of milk protein gives it the smoother, creamier texture normally associated with goat's cheese.

- Sheep only have two teats and produce much less milk than cows, but their milk contains much more fat, protein and minerals, making it ideal for cheesemaking. These higher levels of nutrients means that a sheep's milk cheese requires less milk than an equivalent cow's milk cheese, thereby making it ideal for small farms.

- Buffalo were probably first introduced to Europe by the Roman Empire, who brought them back from their expeditions. The milk contains lower cholesterol but 100 per cent more fat, making it richer and creamier than cow's milk.

- Goat's, sheep's and buffalo's milk can be used to make cheeses in many of the sections in this book but for clarity have been given their own sections.

How Cheese is Made: A Simple Guide

Milk is the nutrient-rich liquid food produced by mammals that contains five key components – water, protein (casein), fat (butterfat), lactose and calcium.

The first stage in the process is to add a bacterial starter culture to feed on the lactose and convert it to lactic acid. This acidification process starts to curdle the milk and raise the acidity. Selection of the starter culture is a key factor in determining the style of cheese that will be produced.

Once the lactic acid has risen to the right level, an enzyme called rennet is added which reacts with the casein protein and causes it to precipitate. As it starts to solidify, it traps the butterfats, calcium and lactic acid within the protein matrix, forming what is known as curd.

The cheesemaker judges when the curd is sufficiently set and releases the liquid whey, which is drained off and can be used for a variety of purposes, such as animal feed, whey powder or whey butter.

The remaining curd is cut into small pieces, the size of which will determine the hardness of the cheese, allowing even more whey to drain from the increased surface area of the curd.

Depending on the cheese style being made, the curd can be treated in a number of ways, such as heating it to change the protein structure further, stacking it when making Cheddar-style cheeses, or adding a bacterial mould to form a soft, white rind or to allow the development of blue veins.

The finished curd, which usually has salt added as a natural preservative and flavouring, is then placed into a shaped mould. As the curd settles in the mould, more whey drains away through gravity pressing the curd down on itself, and in the case of some harder cheeses can be mechanically pressed.

After a time, dependent upon the size of the cheese and the texture required, the partly set cheese is removed from the mould and after any salting, rubbing or other processes used, is put aside to start its maturing and ripening.

This is a very brief and basic summary of the process of cheesemaking, which will be referred to in the descriptions of cheeses in the recipes, but there are a few more terms that will prove useful in understanding how cheese is made.

Cheesemaking Terms

Organic Milk – Definitions of organic vary around the world, but in Britain, the Soil Association sets the standards which can be summarised as follows . . .

Organic cows are fed a grass-rich diet for at least two hundred days per annum, free from artificial additives, chemicals or genetically modified ingredients, and no routine use of antibiotics.

Treatment of Milk – Pasteurised milk has undergone a process of heating to kill all the naturally occurring bacteria and enzymes. The process is designed to kill off any detrimental bacteria but in doing so kills everything. Pasteurisation is usually undertaken when milk from more than one source is used, as any traceability is impossible in the event of a problem. Some cheeses have regulations that prohibit the use of unpasteurised milk, e.g. Stilton. To distinguish it from other processes, pasteurisation involves heating the milk to 72°C for 15 seconds or heating it to 63°C for 30 minutes.

Thermised milk has been heated to between 57°C and 68°C for at least 15 seconds. This process kills some, but not all, of the natural bacteria and enzymes in the milk, thereby retaining more of the natural flavours.

Unpasteurised milk refers to all milk that is not, by definition, pasteurised.

Rennet – Rennet is an essential part of the cheesemaking process as it is used to coagulate the milk and set the curd into a solid form. It was probably discovered by accident when the only method of transporting or storing liquids was an animal's stomach.

Traditional rennet, sometimes referred to as animal rennet, is an enzyme obtained from the stomach lining of an unweaned veal calf. Kid or lamb can also be used.

Vegetarian rennet can be made either by using moulds that produce enzymes that are similar to rennet, or by genetically modifying moulds to produce the rennet enzyme called *Chymosin*.

It's all About the Bread

Although all the recipes in this book use only British cheeses, there are a number of international bread styles in Britain that serve as excellent pairings for different cheeses.

Baguette – The popularity of long sticks of bread in France started in the eighteenth century, using a highly milled flour. The first recorded use of the word 'baguette' to describe bread was in 1920 when a set of laws was published.

The crusty, crisp nature of a baguette pairs well with soft cheeses including soft, white cheeses and soft, rind-washed cheeses.

Ciabatta – This is a relatively recent style of bread, having been invented in 1982 and introduced to Britain in 1985. It was first made in Italy as a response to the growing popularity of French baguettes being used to make sandwiches.

It is made with a soft, wet dough using a high-gluten wheat flour and olive oil. Despite regional variations, it is always dusted with flour after baking, has a crisp, hard crust and a dense crumb with an open texture and large air holes throughout.

The crispness of ciabatta bread makes it perfect for soft, creamy cheeses, including buffalo's milk cheeses.

Crusty White Bloomer – A traditional loaf made from white flour with a soft, crumbly centre and a hard crust. It is cooked directly on the floor of the oven and therefore has a flat base. The soft crust holds the shape of the loaf and the fact that no bread tin is used means that it spreads and blooms, developing a traditional cushion-type shape.

Ideal with virtually any cheeses, crusty white bloomer goes especially well with Cheddar, other firm cheeses and all kinds of rarebit.

Crusty White Farmhouse – A rustic style of loaf with a strong crust, a less uniform crumb and a strong yeasty flavour. Baking in a tin gives the bread straight sides with a spreading top where it spills over the top of the tin and is often split and dusted with flour.

Ideal with virtually any cheeses, crusty white farmhouse goes especially well with Cheddar, other firm cheeses and all kinds of rarebit.

Granary – Made with brown malted flour and malted wheat grains to give a dark crumb and a soft crust. It keeps longer than many other breads with the malted content giving it a smoky sweetness.

Granary bread has a distinctive nutty flavour that pairs well with the nuttiness of Red Leicester, and its sweetness contrasts well with the tanginess of blue cheeses.

Rye – Made with rye flour, which can range from light to very dark brown, rye bread contains more dietary fibre and has a lower glycaemic index (GI) than most breads. The texture is very dense and it is full-flavoured. Rye bread can sometimes be difficult to find and is usually expensive, so granary provides a suitable alternative.

Rye bread is a perfect accompaniment to blue cheeses and other full-flavoured cheeses, such as nutty Red Leicester.

Soda – Soda bread is made by using bicarbonate of soda (sodium bicarbonate) instead of yeast as a raising agent. The traditional ingredients used in soda bread are flour, bicarbonate of soda, salt and buttermilk. The buttermilk contains lactic acid, which reacts with the bicarbonate of soda to form tiny bubbles of carbon dioxide, which causes the raising. It has a firm crumb with a light, cake-like texture and a natural sweetness.

Soda bread is an ideal partner for tangy, strong cheeses.

Sourdough – Made with a fermented starter of flour, water and naturally occurring bacteria instead of baker's yeast, causing lactic acid to form, which creates a sour taste. It has a thick, hard crust with a soft, chewy crumb that lasts longer than most other breads.

The savouriness of sourdough pairs well with many full-flavoured cheeses, including pungent, washed-rind cheeses, as well as feta-style cheeses and other sheep's and goat's milk cheeses.

Spelt – Spelt is an ancient variety of wheat, approximately 9,000 years old, that was cultivated by most ancient civilisations. It went out of favour at the end of the nineteenth century when conventional wheat took over. In the mid 1980s, it was rediscovered in Europe, and, due to its nutritional qualities, became very popular. It is lower in gluten than wheat and is therefore easier to digest.

The nutty flavour of spelt bread pairs well with pungent cheeses, fruity, alpine-style cheeses and any smoked cheeses.

Wholemeal – With a rougher texture than white flour, brown wholemeal flour is the finely ground meal of the grains of whole wheat. It uses all of the grain with the bran husk and germ being retained during processing, making it higher in fibre, coarser in texture and more nutritious than white flour. Toasting makes the natural nuttiness of the bread even more pronounced.

The sweet nuttiness of wholemeal bread makes it an ideal partner for salty blue cheeses and Cheshire.

Notes About the Recipes

Each recipe recommends a specific cheese, many of which are traditionally made artisan cheeses. Alternative cheeses are listed at the end of each recipe that can be used if you are either unable to source a particular cheese or wish to try something different. If, however, you are unable to source an artisan cheese for a recipe, please feel free to use whatever cheese you fancy instead. Every British supermarket has a range of cheeses that are made especially for them (some are traditionally made and others are commercially made), some of which are excellent cheeses.

Although each recipe recommends a particular type of bread, if you have any particular preference or food allergy or intolerance, feel free to use a different bread and experiment. The recipes are based on my own experiences and tastes, so please modify, add, subtract, alter, amend and change as you wish – the process of experimentation is half the fun. The other half is, of course, the tasting, or more correctly, the eating.

There is no such thing as a standard-sized slice of bread and, therefore, exact quantities are difficult to gauge. Each recipe has been based on a large slice of bread (thick-cut or medium-cut, depending on the recipe), either 15 × 15cm or 22 × 10cm, except in the case of recipes using baguette or ciabatta where a 15cm length of bread is cut in half lengthways.

Each recipe makes one serving, but all recipes can easily be doubled up (or more) to make extra servings, if required.

In each recipe, the ingredients are listed in the order in which they are used in the method, with the two most important elements, the **cheese** and the **bread**, being presented in bold typeface so you can easily identify them.

Some recipes recommend specific named brands of cheese. They have been recommended based on flavour during recipe testing and, in some cases, based on geographical relevance. In each case, there are other similar cheese brands available, which you may prefer to use instead.

During testing, I used a separate oven and grill, but some readers may have a combined oven/grill set-up. When assembling a cheese on toast, many of the ingredients and specifically the cheese are usually taken from the fridge and are therefore cold at the time of assembly. If you simply grill the finished item, it is easy to have a beautifully grilled dish that is still cold in the centre. If you only use the oven, the temperature and melt are achieved, but then without the 'browning' from the grill, the visual impact can be rather 'beige'. This was something that I discovered very early on when selling cheese on toast in my shop/restaurant, hence I recommend using a preheated oven and a medium-hot grill to achieve the best results. It is best not to turn the grill up to full/high as this can result in the cheese on toast burning rather than grilling. All grills vary in temperature so I suggest experimenting a bit to find the ideal setting for yours. If you have a combined oven and grill, for preheating purposes, please refer to the manufacturer's guidance.

The recipes specify that the bread should be toasted (on both sides), but individual preference will dictate how much or how little the bread is toasted.

Every recipe has been tried and tested by myself and by many of my friends and family, who have had to put up with the testing stage – it's a tough life!

CHEDDAR

Cheddar originally comes from the village of the same name in Somerset, England, where they have been making cheese since the twelfth century, but it wasn't until the sixteenth century that the cheese made in this area became widely known as Cheddar.

In the seventeenth century, Queen Elizabeth I herself noted that 'West of Wales, just below the Mendip Hills, is the town of Cheddar, known for the excellent and prodigious cheeses made there'. Produced according to a method used to make the French cheese Cantal, Cheddar's name was associated with its town of origin early on. Originally Cheddar had to be made within 30 miles of Wells Cathedral in order to use the name.

Cheddar-making in Somerset goes back more than eight hundred years with records noting that in 1170 King Henry II purchased 10,240 lb (4,644 kg) of Cheddar cheese at a cost of a farthing a pound, and declared Cheddar cheese to be the best in Britain. His son John clearly thought the same, as there are records of him continuing to buy the cheese for the great Royal banquets. In the reign of Charles I, parliamentary records show that the cheese made in Cheddar was sold before it was even made and was only available at the court.

Scott of the Antarctic took with him 3,527 lb (1,600 kg) of Cheddar on his famous expedition in 1901.

Queen Victoria was once presented with a drum of Cheddar that weighed 11 hundredweight (558kg), made using milk from over 700 cows.

Over the centuries, this type of cheese spread across the world, and without any regulations covering either the method of manufacture or the style of the cheese, the name Cheddar became used for pretty much any firm cheese. For example, in the United States, any cheese with a moisture content of up to 39 per cent and at least 50 per cent fat in dry matter can legally be called Cheddar, no matter how it is made or what it looks like.

In earlier times, Cheddar's flavour was often masked by undesirable bacteria, which developed because milk could not be refrigerated. In 1857, Joseph Harding standardised the process known as 'cheddaring' and succeeded in suppressing the growth of the microorganisms.

Cheddaring is a process of rapid acidification achieved by stacking and turning the curds at high temperature during draining. This results in a stringy texture, not unlike white chicken meat. The curds are then ground down into small bits and salted to stop the acidification and remove the whey, thereby lowering the moisture content and adding to the flavour of the cheese.

It is only Cheddars that are made using this traditional method that feature in this book, all of which are handmade according to a strict set of guidelines. In 1994, cheesemakers from the South West of England applied for and were granted Protected Designation of Origin (PDO) for 'West Country Farmhouse Cheddar'. To achieve PDO status, a variety of conditions have to be met, including:

— Made using milk from local herds reared and milked in the counties of Somerset, Dorset, Devon or

Cornwall. The milk may be either unpasteurised or pasteurised.

— Contains no colourings, flavourings or preservatives.

— Made by hand using the traditional method known as 'cheddaring'.

— Made and matured on the farm and aged for at least nine months.

Of the PDO producers, four have been designated as Artisan Somerset Cheddar by Slow Food. They are Montgomery's, Westcombe, Keen's and Pitchfork. There are, however, other excellent traditionally handmade Cheddars, and although they do not meet the Slow Food or PDO criteria, they do still feature in the recipes.

For example, Quicke's meets virtually all of the PDO requirements, but they believe that by scalding the milk at a higher temperature they retain better moisture in their cheese and therefore cannot register it as a PDO cheese. Isle of Mull and Hafod are both excellent Cheddars, but being outside of the West Country they are not eligible for the PDO. Lincolnshire Poacher is not 'cheddared' so isn't strictly a Cheddar, but is sufficiently similar to be included in this section, plus it is an outstanding cheese.

Cheddar is a highly versatile cheese that will work with most styles of bread, but the all-round best combination is a thick slice of crusty, soft, white bread such as a bloomer or a farmhouse – a thick slice is recommended as the bread is soft and will squash down a little during cooking. All the recipes in this section use these styles except for the Isle of Mull Cheddar with Whisky-soaked Haggis recipe, where a rye or granary bread is recommended because the intense boozy flavours of the cheese and haggis need something stronger.

Amazing Cheese on Toast with Montgomery's Cheddar

Jamie Montgomery is the third generation of the Montgomery family which has been hand-making Cheddar for over 100 years at Manor Farm in North Cadbury, Somerset. Made from unpasteurised milk from their own herd of Holstein-Friesian cows with traditional rennet, the cheeses are aged for 12–18 months, during which time they take on a dry, crumbly texture. They develop an intense, full-bodied flavour, which is rich, nutty and slightly sweet.

The deep flavours of Montgomery's Cheddar make it an ideal partner for tangy onions as shown in this recipe. Montgomery's Cheddar is available as either mature or extra mature, which has a more intense flavour. Either is suitable for this recipe.

Ingredients

1 thick slice of crusty white bloomer or farmhouse bread

2 tablespoons caramelised onion chutney (see Tip)

75g Montgomery's Cheddar cheese, grated

1 spring onion, thinly sliced

1 tablespoon crème fraîche

Method

- ❖ Preheat the oven to 180°C/160°C fan/gas 4.

- ❖ Toast the bread on both sides and then place on a small baking tray.

- ❖ Spread the onion chutney on one side of the toast.

- ❖ Mix the cheese, spring onion and crème fraîche to a rough paste. Spread the cheese mixture on top of the chutney.

- ❖ Warm through in the oven for a few minutes, then transfer under the medium-hot grill until the cheese is bubbling and starting to brown.

Tip – If you prefer to use another type of chutney, any fruit-based chutney will create a tasty combination.

•

Other cheeses that can be used in this recipe

Artisan Somerset Cheddars
Westcombe, Keen's, Pitchfork

Cheddars
Quicke's, Hafod, Isle of Mull, Lincolnshire Poacher

Firm cheeses
Red Leicester, Double Gloucester

Westcombe Cheddar Ploughman's on Toast

Cheddar has been made at Westcombe Farm in Evercreech, Somerset, for over 120 years, with the Calver family joining the business in the 1960s. Tom Calver is now head cheesemaker at this traditional dairy, and continues to make top-quality Cheddar using unpasteurised milk from their own herd of Holstein-Friesian cows and traditional rennet. The handmade cheeses are matured for 12–18 months, developing a softer texture than many other Cheddars. The cheese has a deep, complex flavour with a mellow tang and tastes of citrus, hazelnut and caramel.

The soft caramel flavours make this a perfect cheese to pair with the sharp pickled onions and salty ham to create this recipe, which is based on a traditional ploughman's lunch.

Ingredients

1 thick slice of crusty white bloomer or farmhouse bread

50g slice of your favourite traditional cooked ham

75g Westcombe Cheddar cheese, grated

2 pickled onions, drained and thinly sliced (see Tip)

1 tablespoon crème fraîche

Method

❖ Preheat the oven to 180°C/160°C fan/gas 4.

❖ Toast the bread on both sides and then place on a
small baking tray.

❖ Lay the ham on one side of the toast.

❖ Mix the cheese, pickled onions and crème fraîche to a
rough paste. Spread the cheese mixture on top of the
ham.

❖ Warm through in the oven for a few minutes, then
transfer under the medium-hot grill until the cheesy
topping is bubbling and starting to brown.

Tip – Swap the pickled onions for spring onions for a less
tangy sharpness, if you prefer.

•

Other cheeses that can be used in this recipe

Artisan Somerset Cheddars
Montgomery's, Keen's, Pitchfork

Cheddars
Quicke's, Hafod, Isle of Mull, Lincolnshire Poacher

Firm cheeses
Red Leicester, Double Gloucester

Keen's Cheddar with Mango Chutney and Peach

The Keen family have been hand-making traditional Cheddar at Moorhayes Farm to the north of Wincanton, Somerset, since 1899 and it is now the fifth generation of the family who continue to make this excellent artisan Somerset Cheddar. The cheese is made using unpasteurised milk from their own herd of Holstein-Friesian cows with traditional rennet. It has a dense, rich and creamy texture with a range of flavours from tangy savouriness to juicy nuttiness.

The savoury acidity contrasts perfectly with the sweetness of the peach and the mango chutney. Using slightly sweet soft granary bread instead of the white bread will provide a further taste contrast, if you prefer.

Ingredients

1 thick slice of crusty white bloomer or farmhouse bread

2 teaspoons mango chutney

75g Keen's Cheddar cheese, grated

1 ripe peach, halved, stoned and sliced

Method

❖ Preheat the oven to 180°C/160°C fan/gas 4.

❖ Toast the bread on both sides and then place on a
small baking tray.

❖ Spread the mango chutney on one side of the toast.
Scatter the cheese over the chutney, then place the
peach slices on top.

❖ Warm through in the oven for a few minutes, then
transfer under the medium-hot grill until the cheese is
bubbling and the peach slices are starting to caramelise.

Other cheeses that can be used in this recipe

Artisan Somerset Cheddars
Montgomery's, Westcombe, Pitchfork

Cheddars
Quicke's, Hafod, Isle of Mull, Lincolnshire Poacher

Firm cheeses
Red Leicester, Double Gloucester

Pitchfork Cheddar Waldorf-style

Pitchfork Cheddar is a relatively new cheese compared to the previous ones, all of which have been made for over 100 years. The Trethowan family moved from Wales to Puxton Court Farm near Weston-super-Mare, Somerset, in 2014, but have already created a 'proper old-fashioned Cheddar', which they launched in 2018. Made using unpasteurised, organic milk and traditional rennet, the cheese is full-bodied with a dense, creamy texture and an acidic, juicy bite.

The acidic freshness of the Granny Smith apple and the warm nuttiness of walnuts make an excellent pairing for this cheese. Crusty white bread forms the perfect base for this recipe.

Ingredients

1 thick slice of crusty white bloomer or farmhouse bread

½ Granny Smith apple, peeled, cored and sliced (see Tip)

75g Pitchfork Cheddar cheese, grated

50g walnut pieces

Method

❖ Preheat the oven to 180°C/160°C fan/gas 4.

❖ Toast the bread on both sides and then place on a small baking tray.

❖ Place the apple slices on one side of the toast, then sprinkle the cheese over the top.

❖ Warm through in the oven for a few minutes, then press the walnut pieces into the partially melted cheese.

❖ Place under the medium-hot grill until the cheese is bubbling and starting to brown (being careful not to let the nuts burn).

Tip – Try using ½ pear instead of the apple for a tasty variation.

•

Other cheeses that can be used in this recipe

Artisan Somerset Cheddars
Montgomery's, Westcombe, Keen's

Cheddars
Quicke's, Hafod, Isle of Mull, Lincolnshire Poacher

Firm cheeses
Red Leicester, Double Gloucester

Quicke's Cheddar with Spiced Apple

The Quicke family have been farming at Home Farm in Newton St Cyres, near Exeter in Devon, for nearly 500 years. Mary Quicke is the fourteenth generation to live on the farm and the fifth generation of the family cheesemaking business. Their herd is a hybrid of seven different dairy breeds, including Montbeliarde, Scandinavian Red, Holstein-Friesian and Jersey. All Quicke's Cheddars are made from pasteurised milk using traditional rennet to give a buttery flavour which develops more complexity, bite and umami flavours as it matures. It is available as Mature (12 months), Extra Mature (18 months) or Vintage (24 months), which has the most intense flavour. Any of these are suitable for this recipe, depending on personal taste.

Ingredients

½ Granny Smith apple, peeled, cored and sliced (see Tip)

1 teaspoon light soft brown sugar

½ teaspoon ground cinnamon

½ teaspoon freshly grated or ground nutmeg

2 teaspoons unsalted butter

1 thick slice of crusty white bloomer or farmhouse bread

75g Quicke's Cheddar cheese, grated

Method

❖ Put the apple slices in a small bowl with the sugar and spices and stir to coat the apple. Melt the butter in a small saucepan, add the apple and cook over a low heat for about 10 minutes or until softened, stirring once or twice.

❖ Meanwhile, preheat the grill to medium-high. Toast the bread on both sides and then place on a small baking tray.

❖ Pour the cooked apple onto one side of the toast. Scatter the cheese over the top.

❖ Place under the preheated grill until the cheese is bubbling and starting to brown.

Tip – ½ pear can be substituted for the apple, if you like.

•

Other cheeses that can be used in this recipe

Artisan Somerset Cheddars
Montgomery's, Westcombe, Keen's, Pitchfork

Cheddars
Hafod, Isle of Mull, Lincolnshire Poacher

Firm cheeses
Red Leicester, Double Gloucester

Hafod Cheddar with Leek and Mustard

Hafod, meaning summer pasture in Welsh, is a traditional Cheddar handmade by Sam and Rachel Holden on Wales' longest certified organic dairy farm, Bwlchwernen Fawr, near Lampeter, Ceredigion. Using unpasteurised organic milk from their own herd of Ayrshire cows and traditional rennet, they make this buttery, rich cheese, which is matured for 16 months to develop its full flavour. The original recipe originated with a Swiss-trained cheesemaker and although it is similar to that of a traditional Cheddar, its nutty flavour is also reminiscent of a traditional Alpine cheese.

The sweet and sharp tanginess of the leek retains the Welsh connection and the sharp acidity of the mustard pairs well with this nutty, slightly sweet Cheddar.

Ingredients

20g unsalted butter

5cm piece of leek, washed and thinly sliced

1 teaspoon plain flour

½ teaspoon English mustard powder (see Tip)

50ml full-fat or semi-skimmed milk

50g Hafod Cheddar cheese, grated

1 thick slice of crusty white bloomer or farmhouse bread

Method

❖ Melt the butter in a small saucepan, add the leek and cook gently for about 10 minutes or until softened but not browned, stirring occasionally.

❖ Add the flour and mustard powder, stirring to a thick paste, then stir in the milk and keep stirring over a low heat until it has thickened. Gradually stir in the cheese until it's fully melted and you have a thick sauce.

❖ Meanwhile, preheat the grill to medium-high. Toast the bread on both sides and then place on a small baking tray.

❖ Slowly pour the cheese sauce over one side of the toast.

❖ Place under the preheated grill until the cheesy topping is bubbling and browning in places.

Tip – If you don't have mustard powder to hand, use the same quantity of ready-made English mustard instead.

•

Other cheeses that can be used in this recipe

Artisan Somerset Cheddars
Montgomery's, Westcombe, Keen's, Pitchfork

Cheddars
Quicke's, Isle of Mull, Lincolnshire Poacher

Firm cheeses
Red Leicester, Double Gloucester

Isle of Mull Cheddar with Whisky-soaked Haggis

Isle of Mull Cheddar is made by the Reade family at Sgriob-ruadh farm near Tobermory on the Isle of Mull in Scotland. The Holstein-Friesian cows, whose unpasteurised milk is used with traditional rennet to make the cheese, are fed on fermented grain from the nearby Tobermory whisky distillery. This diet gives the cheese a sharp, fruity tang with a distinctly 'boozy' flavour and rich savouriness.

Given how traditional it is to enjoy a dram of whisky with haggis, I have created this tasty pairing of tangy, boozy Cheddar with slightly sweet, spicy, meaty haggis soaked in whisky. Nutty, slightly sweet rye or granary bread makes the combination irresistible.

Ingredients

50g cooked haggis (see Tips)

1 tablespoon Scotch whisky (see Tips)

1 medium slice of rye or granary bread

1 teaspoon English mustard

75g Isle of Mull Cheddar cheese, grated

Method

❖ Preheat the oven to 180°C/160°C fan/gas 4.

❖ Crumble the haggis into a bowl, pour over the whisky and mix well. Leave to soak for 10 minutes.

❖ Preheat the grill to medium-high. Toast the bread on both sides and then place on a small baking tray.

❖ Spread the mustard onto one side of the toast. Spoon the whisky-soaked haggis over the mustard. Sprinkle the cheese on top.

❖ Warm through in the oven for a few minutes, then transfer under the preheated grill until the cheese is bubbling and starting to brown.

Tips – Swap the haggis for cooked black pudding, and try using brandy instead of whisky, if you like.

•

Other cheeses that can be used in this recipe

Artisan Somerset Cheddars
Montgomery's, Westcombe, Keen's, Pitchfork

Cheddars
Quicke's, Hafod, Lincolnshire Poacher

Firm cheeses
Red Leicester, Double Gloucester

Lincolnshire Poacher with Mustard and Horseradish

Lincolnshire Poacher has been made by Simon and Tim Jones at Ulceby Grange in Alford, Lincolnshire, since 1970. They use unpasteurised milk from their own herd of Holstein-Friesian cows with traditional rennet. The cheese is almost a cross between a traditional West Country Cheddar and an Alpine-style cheese.

The full, slightly sweet, almost pineapple flavours in this cheese pair beautifully with the tangy heat of the mustard and horseradish and the savoury flavour of the sourdough. Lincolnshire Poacher is available as either regular (14–16 months), or vintage (18–22 months) with more depth and complexity. Either is suitable for this recipe, depending on personal taste.

Ingredients

1 medium slice of sourdough bread

1½ teaspoons English wholegrain mustard (see Tips)

1 tablespoon creamed horseradish sauce

75g Lincolnshire Poacher cheese, thinly sliced

2 teaspoons snipped fresh chives (see Tips)

Method

* Preheat the grill to medium-high.

* Toast the bread on both sides and then place on a small baking tray.

* Mix the mustard and horseradish to a smooth paste, then spread this over one side of the toast. Lay the cheese slices on top.

* Place under the preheated grill until the cheese is bubbling and starting to brown.

* Sprinkle the snipped chives on top just before serving.

Tips – If you don't have wholegrain mustard, use French mustard instead, and finely chopped parsley can be swapped in for the chives.

•

Other cheeses that can be used in this recipe

Artisan Somerset Cheddars
Montgomery's, Westcombe, Keen's, Pitchfork

Cheddars
Quicke's, Hafod, Isle of Mull

Firm cheeses
Red Leicester, Double Gloucester

SOFT, WHITE CREAMY CHEESES

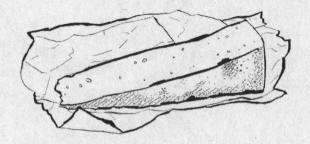

Soft, white cheeses typically have a white rind, a smooth runny texture and a heady aroma of mushrooms. They are sometimes referred to as mould-ripened cheeses and can be made from any milk including cow's, goat's, sheep's or buffalo's. Milder versions smell of white button mushrooms and fresh hay, whilst more mature versions have a stronger earthy mushroom aroma. Soft cheese made with goat's milk has mild tastes of almonds, whereas sheep's milk versions have a slight sweetness with a hint of roast meat.

These cheeses retain a high percentage of whey, which causes their runny texture. This is done by scooping the curds gently into moulds, then the weight of the curd acts to press out the excess whey without any additional pressing. After the curds are turned out of the cheese moulds, they are sprayed with *Penicillium candidum*, which causes the thick white velvety rind and the mushroomy aroma to develop after a few weeks of maturing. It is this thick rind that stops the cheese from drying out and allows the centre to ripen and become soft and creamy. The higher levels of whey result in a lower fat and moisture content than harder cheeses. These cheeses tend to be almost chalky when young, but soften and become creamier as they ripen and mature.

The creamy richness of these cheeses needs a slight sourness in the bread to provide a flavour contrast. Crusty baguette provides a great balance between a tangy sourness and soft, creamy texture in the bread, which pairs excellently with the soft, buttery texture of the cheeses. The only exception is the Triple Rose cheese recipe, which being a triple cream cheese, is super-rich and creamy, therefore tangy soda bread pairs perfectly with it to avoid the cheese dominating.

Waterloo with Roasted Cherries

Waterloo is named after the milk from Guernsey cows on the Duke of Wellington's estate in Berkshire, where the cheese was first made by Anne and Andy Wigmore of Village Maid Cheese. They now make it in their own dairy in nearby Riseley using locally sourced thermised Guernsey milk and vegetarian rennet, which gives the cheese its deep golden colour inside the soft, white rind.

The cheese has a rich, buttery flavour and soft, creamy texture which pairs well with the sourness of the cherries and the sweetness of the maple syrup. The crustiness of the baguette provides a great contrast pairing with the Waterloo cheese.

Ingredients

75g fresh cherries, halved and stoned

2 tablespoons maple syrup

1 teaspoon fresh rosemary leaves, finely chopped

15cm piece of baguette, cut in half lengthways

100g Waterloo cheese, thinly sliced

Method

❖ Preheat the oven to 180°C/160°C fan/gas 4.

❖ Place the cherries in a small baking dish with the maple syrup and rosemary and stir gently to combine. Bake in the oven for about 30 minutes or until the cherries become soft and sticky, stirring a couple of times during cooking.

❖ Preheat the grill to medium-high. Toast the baguette halves on both sides and then place on a small baking tray, cut-sides up.

❖ Lay the cheese slices on the toast, then spoon the roasted cherries over the cheese.

❖ Place under the preheated grill until the cheese has melted and is starting to bubble.

•

Other cheeses that can be used in this recipe

Soft, white cheeses
Bath Soft, Baron Bigod, Perl Wen, Tunworth, Finn, Penyston Brie, Sharpham, Triple Rose, Bix

Soft goat's or sheep's milk cheeses
Golden Cross, Ragstone, Cerney Ash, White Nancy, Wigmore, Flower Marie

Bath Soft with Blackberries

Bath Soft is made by Graham Padfield at Park Farm in Kelston, near Bath, Somerset. The recipe dates back to 1801 when Admiral Lord Nelson allegedly had some of this cheese sent to him by his father. It is made using pasteurised organic milk from their own herd using traditional rennet. The soft, golden cheese is coated with a soft, white rind, similar to a Brie-style cheese and is sold as a square, wrapped in parchment-style paper. When young, the cheese has a fresh, grassy flavour that matures into a creamy texture and develops a mushroomy taste.

The richness of the cheese is complemented by the sweet tanginess and acidity of the blackberries in this recipe.

Ingredients

15cm piece of baguette, cut in half lengthways

50g fresh blackberries (see Tip)

100g Bath Soft cheese, thinly sliced

Method

- ❖ Preheat the grill to medium-high.

- ❖ Toast the baguette halves on both sides and then place on a small baking tray, cut-sides up.

- ❖ Place the blackberries on the toast and gently squash them to release the juices. Lay the slices of cheese on top.

- ❖ Place under the preheated grill until the cheese has melted and is starting to bubble.

Tip – If fresh blackberries are not in season, use 50g of blackberry or bramble conserve or jam instead. Simply spread it evenly over the toast and top with the cheese, then grill as above.

•

Other cheeses that can be used in this recipe

Soft, white cheeses
Waterloo, Baron Bigod, Perl Wen, Tunworth, Finn, Penyston Brie, Sharpham, Triple Rose, Bix

Soft goat's or sheep's milk cheeses
Golden Cross, Ragstone, Cerney Ash, White Nancy, Wigmore, Flower Marie

Baron Bigod with Balsamic Beetroot

Baron Bigod is made by Jonny and Dulcie Crickmore at Fen Farm Dairy, near Bungay in Suffolk. This creamy, white-rinded cheese is made from unpasteurised Montbeliarde cow's milk from their own herd using traditional rennet. The cheese has a smooth, silky texture and a golden curd, with long-lasting, warm, earthy farmyard and mushroom flavours. It is the only unpasteurised Brie de Meaux-style cheese made in Britain, using a traditional French recipe. The cheese is hand-ladled into moulds, hand-salted, then matured for eight weeks in a cave-like environment.

The sweet sharpness of the balsamic vinegar and sweet earthiness of the beetroot pair beautifully with the creamy richness of the cheese.

Ingredients

1 tablespoon olive oil

1 medium raw beetroot, peeled and thinly sliced

1 tablespoon balsamic vinegar

1 teaspoon fresh thyme leaves (see Tips)

15cm piece of baguette, cut in half lengthways

100g Baron Bigod cheese, thinly sliced

Method

❖ Preheat the grill to medium-high.

❖ Heat the olive oil in a small frying pan over a medium heat, add the beetroot slices, balsamic vinegar and thyme leaves and sauté for about 10 minutes or until the beetroot is tender.

❖ Meanwhile, toast the baguette halves on both sides and then place on a small baking tray, cut-sides up.

❖ Arrange the beetroot slices on the toast, pour over any juices and lay the cheese slices on top.

❖ Place under the preheated grill until the cheese has melted and is starting to bubble.

Tips – Use ½ teaspoon dried thyme instead of fresh, or try using 1 teaspoon finely chopped tarragon, oregano or rosemary instead of the thyme.

•

Other cheeses that can be used in this recipe

Soft, white cheeses
Waterloo, Bath Soft, Perl Wen, Tunworth, Finn, Penyston Brie, Sharpham, Triple Rose, Bix

Soft goat's or sheep's milk cheeses
Golden Cross, Ragstone, Cerney Ash, White Nancy, Wigmore, Flower Marie

Perl Wen with Cranberry Sauce

Perl Wen, Welsh for white pearl, is made by Carwyn Adams at Caws Cenarth on Glyneithinog Farm in Carmarthenshire, Wales. It is made from pasteurised organic milk using vegetarian rennet and is described as a cross between Caerphilly and Brie. This is because the cheese is made to the family's Caerphilly base recipe but is then mould-ripened like a Brie for seven weeks. The soft, white rind yields easily to reveal a mellow yellow centre, which is creamy and rich with a hint of citrus freshness and salty tanginess.

Here, the sharp, tangy sweetness of the cranberry sauce partners well with the citrusy creaminess of the cheese.

Ingredients

15cm piece of baguette, cut in half lengthways

50g cranberry sauce (see Tip)

100g Perl Wen cheese, thinly sliced

Method

❖ Preheat the grill to medium-high.

❖ Toast the baguette halves on both sides and then place on a small baking tray, cut-sides up.

❖ Spread the cranberry sauce on the toast. Lay the cheese slices on top.

❖ Place under the preheated grill until the cheese has melted and is starting to bubble.

Tip – Raspberry jam is a good alternative to cranberry sauce in this recipe.

●

Other cheeses that can be used in this recipe

Soft, white cheeses
Waterloo, Bath Soft, Baron Bigod, Tunworth, Finn, Penyston Brie, Sharpham, Triple Rose, Bix

Soft goat's or sheep's milk cheeses
Golden Cross, Ragstone, Cerney Ash, White Nancy, Wigmore, Flower Marie

Tunworth with Roasted Garlic, Rosemary and Honey

Stacey Hedges is an Australian cheese lover who travelled the world before settling in Hampshire, where she made trial batches of cheese in her own kitchen. Soon after, she met up with Charlotte Spruce and together they formed Hampshire Cheeses on the Herriard Estate, close to Basingstoke, and started making the artisan handmade cheese known as Tunworth. Pasteurised milk from a local farm is used with traditional rennet. Based on French Camembert, but smoother, creamier and richer, Tunworth is the same size and shape as its French cousin and even comes in a similar round wooden box.

The richness of the cheese is complemented by the sweetness of the garlic and honey and the aromatic sharpness of the rosemary.

Ingredients

2 garlic cloves, peeled

1 tablespoon runny honey

1 teaspoon fresh rosemary leaves, finely chopped

15cm piece of baguette, cut in half lengthways

100g Tunworth cheese, thinly sliced

Method

❖ Preheat the oven to 180°C/160°C fan/gas 4.

❖ Place the garlic cloves, honey and rosemary leaves in a small ovenproof dish, and stir to mix. Cover with foil and roast in the oven for about 30 minutes or until the garlic is soft when pressed with the back of a teaspoon.

❖ Preheat the grill to medium-high. Toast the baguette halves on both sides and then place on a small baking tray, cut-sides up.

❖ Mash the garlic, honey and rosemary into a soft paste, then spread half of this over the toast. Lay the cheese slices on top, then dot the remaining garlic paste over the top.

❖ Place under the preheated grill until the cheese has melted and is starting to bubble.

•

Other cheeses that can be used in this recipe

Soft, white cheeses
Waterloo, Bath Soft, Baron Bigod, Perl Wen, Finn, Penyston Brie, Sharpham, Triple Rose, Bix

Soft goat's or sheep's milk cheeses
Golden Cross, Ragstone, Cerney Ash, White Nancy, Wigmore, Flower Marie

Finn with Kiwi Fruit

Finn is made by Charlie Westhead of Neal's Yard Creamery in Dorstone, Herefordshire. The name is Irish for 'great white one' and it is named after Charlie's dog. It is made using pasteurised organic milk from Holstein-Friesian cows and vegetarian rennet. Finn is a triple cream cheese, based on French cheeses such as Brillat Savarin and Délice. Enriching the milk with extra cream before making the cheese gives a decadent silky richness and creamy texture.

The luxurious creamy texture of the cheese pairs well with the sweet tanginess of the kiwi fruit in this delicious recipe.

Ingredients

15cm piece of baguette, cut in half lengthways

1 kiwi fruit, peeled and thinly sliced

100g Finn cheese, thinly sliced

Method

❖ Preheat the grill to medium-high.

❖ Toast the baguette halves on both sides and then place on a small baking tray, cut-sides up.

❖ Arrange the kiwi slices on the toast and lay the cheese slices over the top.

❖ Place under the preheated grill until the cheese has melted and is starting to bubble.

Other cheeses that can be used in this recipe

Soft, white cheeses
Waterloo, Bath Soft, Baron Bigod, Perl Wen, Tunworth, Penyston Brie, Sharpham, Triple Rose, Bix

Soft goat's or sheep's milk cheeses
Golden Cross, Ragstone, Cerney Ash, White Nancy, Wigmore, Flower Marie

Penyston Brie with Pear and Honey

Peter Kindel and the team at Daylesford Farm in Kingham, Gloucestershire, make Penyston Brie using unpasteurised organic milk from their own herd of Gloucester and Holstein-Friesian cows and vegetarian rennet. Five weeks' maturing allows the soft, white rind to develop and the centre to become soft, oozy, creamy and buttery. The cheese has a buttery and mushroomy flavour that develops further as it matures.

The gentle acidity of the pear works well with this cheese to give a light but flavoursome combination.

Ingredients

15cm piece of baguette, cut in half lengthways

100g Penyston Brie cheese, thinly sliced

1 pear, cored and thinly sliced

2 teaspoons runny honey

Method

- ❖ Preheat the grill to medium-high.

- ❖ Toast the baguette halves on both sides and then place on a small baking tray, cut-sides up.

- ❖ Arrange the cheese slices on the toast, top with the pear slices, then drizzle over the honey.

- ❖ Place under the preheated grill until the cheese has melted and is starting to bubble and the pear slices have started to lightly brown.

Other cheeses that can be used in this recipe

Soft, white cheeses
Waterloo, Bath Soft, Baron Bigod, Perl Wen, Tunworth, Finn, Sharpham, Triple Rose, Bix

Soft goat's or sheep's milk cheeses
Golden Cross, Ragstone, Cerney Ash, White Nancy, Wigmore, Flower Marie

Sharpham Mexican-style

Made on the Sharpham Estate on the banks of the River Dart, near Totnes in Devon, by Greg and Nicky Parsons and the team, this cheese is often described as a Brie, but is actually closer to a French Coulommier. Handmade using unpasteurised Jersey milk and vegetarian rennet, it has a unique, meltingly soft, creamy texture and buttery flavour.

The creamy delicacy of the cheese pairs beautifully with the soft, creamy avocado and the tangy lime, with the chilli providing a tongue-tingling contrast to the creaminess.

Ingredients

15cm piece of baguette, cut in half lengthways

1 avocado, peeled, stoned and mashed

finely grated zest and juice of 1 lime

½ teaspoon sea salt

½ fresh red chilli, deseeded and finely chopped

100g Sharpham cheese, thinly sliced

Method

❖ Preheat the grill to medium-high.

❖ Toast the baguette halves on both sides and then place on a small baking tray, cut-sides up.

❖ Mix the avocado, lime zest and juice and sea salt in a bowl. Spread the avocado mix on the toast, then sprinkle with the chilli. Lay the cheese slices on top.

❖ Place under the preheated grill until the cheese has melted and is starting to bubble.

Other cheeses that can be used in this recipe

Soft, white cheeses
Waterloo, Bath Soft, Baron Bigod, Perl Wen, Tunworth, Finn, Penyston Brie, Triple Rose, Bix

Soft goat's or sheep's milk cheeses
Golden Cross, Ragstone, Cerney Ash, White Nancy, Wigmore, Flower Marie

Triple Rose with Pecans and Rosemary

Dean Wright of Ballylisk makes Triple Rose cheese using milk from his family's herd of Holstein-Friesians on their farm in Tandragee, County Armagh, Northern Ireland. The pasteurised milk is transported just a few miles to the dairy in nearby Portadown. Vegetarian rennet and extra cream are added to the curds to create this triple cream cheese. The soft, white rind surrounds a luxuriously decadent soft cheese with a rich, creamy texture and buttery, salty flavours with a citrusy taste.

The sweet nuttiness of the pecans and the aromatic sharpness of the rosemary pair well with the soft creaminess of the cheese. Creamy, buttermilk-based soda bread provides a perfect base for this recipe, as well as retaining the strong Irish connection.

Ingredients

1 medium slice of soda bread

75g Triple Rose cheese

50g pecan nuts, chopped (see Tip)

1 Amaretti biscuit, crumbled

1 teaspoon demerara sugar

1 teaspoon finely chopped fresh rosemary

Method

❖ Preheat the grill to medium-high.

❖ Toast the bread on both sides and then place on a small baking tray.

❖ Spread the cheese over one side of the toast.

❖ Mix the pecans, biscuit, sugar and rosemary together. Sprinkle the mixture over the cheese.

❖ Place under the preheated grill until the cheese has melted and is starting to bubble and the nut mixture is starting to turn light brown (being careful not to let it burn).

Tip – Try swapping in blanched almonds for the pecans.

•

Other cheeses that can be used in this recipe

Soft, white cheeses
Waterloo, Bath Soft, Baron Bigod, Perl Wen, Tunworth, Finn, Penyston Brie, Sharpham, Bix

Soft goat's or sheep's milk cheeses
Golden Cross, Ragstone, Cerney Ash, White Nancy, Wigmore, Flower Marie

Bix with Fig, Orange and Pistachios

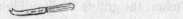

Made by Rose Grimond and her team at Nettlebed Creamery near Henley-on-Thames in South Oxfordshire, this triple cream cheese is based on classic French cheeses like Chaource or Brillat Savarin. Using organic pasteurised milk and traditional rennet, the texture is dense, rich and buttery with yogurty flavours and hints of clover and meadow grass. The soft rind has an earthy aroma and flavour.

The richness of the cheese pairs beautifully with the rich sweetness of the fig, whilst the sweet tanginess of the orange and the nuttiness of the pistachios provide additional flavour and texture.

Ingredients

15cm piece of baguette, cut in half lengthways

1 fresh ripe fig, peeled and chopped

25g pistachios, chopped

½ small orange, peeled, segmented and chopped

100g Bix cheese, thinly sliced

Method

- ❖ Preheat the grill to medium-high.

- ❖ Toast the baguette halves on both sides and then place on a small baking tray, cut-sides up.

- ❖ Combine the fig, pistachios and orange. Spread the fig mixture on the toast. Lay the cheese slices on top.

- ❖ Place under the preheated grill until the cheese has melted and is starting to bubble.

•

Other cheeses that can be used in this recipe

Soft, white cheeses
Waterloo, Bath Soft, Baron Bigod, Perl Wen, Tunworth, Finn, Penyston Brie, Sharpham, Triple Rose

Soft goat's or sheep's milk cheeses
Golden Cross, Ragstone, Cerney Ash, White Nancy, Wigmore, Flower Marie

RED LEICESTER

Named after the city of the same name, Leicester cheese was originally made using milk left over from Stilton production, which was made in the same area. Originally known as just 'Leicestershire', it can be traced back to the seventeenth century, when virtually every county in England made its own distinctive cheese. It was influenced by the southern Cheddar and northern Cheshire and is said by some to be a cross between them.

The red colour was used to distinguish it from cheeses from neighbouring counties and was created using annatto, a natural vegetable colouring extracted from a South American fruit. Annatto had already started being used in Gloucestershire and Cheshire, but Leicestershire used it to a greater extent and developed a deeper red colour.

The city of Leicester established a cheese market in 1759 and it quickly became the main place for buying and selling the cheese, so it introduced rules and regulations governing the quality of the cheeses. As a result, the cheese became known as 'Leicester' after the city rather than the county.

During the Second World War, demand for liquid milk grew and in order to conserve it, production of speciality cheeses was banned along with the use of colourings. All cheeses had to be made to a national recipe, officially referred to as Government Cheddar. Leicestershire people usually called it White Leicester. At the end of wartime, when rationing was ended in the early 1950s, production of the traditional cheese was resumed, and so to avoid confusion became known as Red Leicester.

In the following years, traditional farmhouse cheese-making started declining with the rise of large national dairies making cheeses in centralised locations, often a distance from their traditional counties, in block form. In the past 20 years, falling milk prices have led to a revival of traditional cheesemaking and there are now several producers of farmhouse Red Leicester, handmade and wrapped in cloth before being matured for 6–12 months.

The maturing results in a crumbly texture and a nutty, caramel flavour with a citrus finish.

The flavour of Red Leicester demands a deeper and more complex bread with tastes to match the intensity of the cheese. The nuttiness of a rye or granary bread works best with these recipes and is used in all of them, but if you prefer a milder flavour of bread, then wholemeal is recommended.

Sparkenhoe Red Leicester with Branston Pickle

Made by David and Jo Clarke and their son Will and daughter Annie at Sparkenhoe Farm near Upton, Leicestershire, this is a traditional farmhouse Red Leicester. Unpasteurised milk from their herd of Holstein-Friesian cows and traditional rennet is used to make this clothbound, red-coloured cheese. The texture is hard and crumbly but with a moist chewiness.

Branston Pickle is recommended for this recipe due to its rich fruitiness and the fact that it was originally made in nearby Burton on Trent. Rich, nutty, citrus flavours make this a delicious cheese to pair with the sweet tanginess of the pickle and the nuttiness of the rye or granary bread.

Ingredients

1 medium slice of rye or granary bread

2 tablespoons Branston Pickle (see Tip)

75g Sparkenhoe Red Leicester cheese, grated

1 spring onion, thinly sliced

1 tablespoon crème fraîche

Method

- ❖ Preheat the oven to 180°C/160°C fan/gas 4.

- ❖ Toast the bread on both sides and then place on a small baking tray.

- ❖ Spread the pickle on one side of the toast.

- ❖ Mix the cheese, spring onion and crème fraîche to a rough paste. Spread over the pickle.

- ❖ Warm through in the oven for a few minutes, then transfer under the medium-hot grill until the cheese has melted and is starting to brown.

Tip – Branston Pickle is top choice for this recipe, but other similar pickles will also work well.

•

Other cheeses that can be used in this recipe

Red Leicesters
Hoe Stevenson Rutland Red, Devonshire Red, Red Fox

Firm cheeses
Double Gloucester

Crumbly cheeses
Lancashire, Cheshire, Wensleydale

Hoe Stevenson Rutland Red: Red Nose Day

Thomas Hoe Stevenson was one of the original cheese-makers in the Vale of Belvoir and it is after him that this cheese is named. It is made by Long Clawson Dairy in the village of the same name near Melton Mowbray, Leicestershire. Pasteurised milk is sourced from local farms that have supplied them for generations and vegetarian rennet is used to make the cheese. The firm, moist and crumbly texture is complemented by a tangy, creamy, nutty flavour with hints of caramel.

These flavours were selected to make this themed recipe, first made to celebrate Red Nose Day, by using all red ingredients with high acidity to pair with the natural sweetness of the cheese.

Ingredients

1 medium slice of rye or granary bread

75g Hoe Stevenson Rutland Red cheese, grated

½ small red onion, thinly sliced

½ tomato

Method

❖ Preheat the oven to 180°C/160°C fan/gas 4.

❖ Toast the bread on both sides and then place on a small baking tray.

❖ Scatter the cheese over one side of the toast. Sprinkle the red onion on top, then place the tomato half, cut-side down, in the middle of the cheese to create the 'red nose'.

❖ Warm through in the oven for a few minutes, then transfer under the medium-hot grill until the cheese has melted and is starting to brown (be careful not to let the tomato burn).

Other cheeses that can be used in this recipe

Red Leicesters
Sparkenhoe, Devonshire Red, Red Fox

Firm cheeses
Double Gloucester

Crumbly cheeses
Lancashire, Cheshire, Wensleydale

Devonshire Red with Pilchards and Tomato

Although famed for the award-winning Cheddar that her family originally created, Mary Quicke and the team at Home Farm in Devon have also created other styles of British cheeses. This modern-style cheese is Quicke's take on traditional Red Leicester, clothbound and matured for six months. They use pasteurised milk from their own herd and vegetarian rennet. It has a crumbly but creamy texture with fresh, nutty and slightly sweet flavours.

This unusual pairing of the cheese with pilchards is a flavour sensation, complemented by the acidity of the tomato.

Ingredients

1 medium slice of rye or granary bread

½ × 155g can (75g) pilchards in tomato sauce (see Tip)

75g Quicke's Devonshire Red cheese, grated

1 tomato, thinly sliced

Method

❖ Preheat the oven to 180°C/160°C fan/gas 4.

❖ Toast the bread on both sides and then place on a small baking tray.

❖ Arrange the pilchards and any tomato sauce on one side of the toast.

❖ Scatter the cheese over the pilchards. Lay the tomato slices on top.

❖ Warm through in the oven for a few minutes, then transfer under the medium-hot grill until the cheese has melted and the cheese and tomato slices are starting to lightly brown.

Tip – Try using canned sardines in place of the pilchards, for a change.

•

Other cheeses that can be used in this recipe

Red Leicesters
Sparkenhoe, Hoe Stevenson Rutland Red, Red Fox

Firm cheeses
Double Gloucester

Crumbly cheeses
Lancashire, Cheshire, Wensleydale

Red Fox with Tuna, Onion and Greek Yogurt

The Beckett family have farmed at Belton Farm in Whitchurch, Shropshire, for three generations but have recently developed this unique modern cheese. The cheese is made using pasteurised milk from local farms with vegetarian rennet. The recipe is based on an aged Red Leicester, but this cheese is matured for 16 months, during which time crystals of calcium lactate develop to give a distinctive crunch to the cheese whilst retaining a moist creaminess. It has both sweet and savoury nutty flavours as well as a refreshing citrus taste.

The complex flavours of this cheese work well with this unusual pairing of tuna and tangy onion combined with rich, creamy Greek yogurt.

Ingredients

1 medium slice of rye or granary bread

60g (drained weight) canned tuna chunks in spring water

1 tablespoon Greek yogurt

½ red onion, finely chopped

75g Red Fox cheese, thinly sliced

Method

❖ Preheat the oven to 180°C/160°C fan/gas 4.

❖ Toast the bread on both sides and then place on a small baking tray.

❖ Mix together the tuna, yogurt and onion. Spread this over one side of the toast. Lay the cheese slices on top.

❖ Warm through in the oven for a few minutes, then transfer under the medium-hot grill until the cheese has melted and is starting to brown.

•

Other cheeses that can be used in this recipe

Red Leicesters
Sparkenhoe, Hoe Stevenson Rutland Red, Devonshire Red

Firm cheeses
Double Gloucester

Crumbly cheeses
Lancashire, Cheshire, Wensleydale

DOUBLE GLOUCESTER

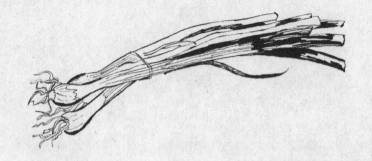

Gloucester cheese has been made in the county of the same name since the sixteenth century, originally using milk from Gloucester cattle, a traditional breed that very nearly became extinct in the 1970s. There are two types of cheese, Single Gloucester and Double Gloucester, with the single variety being mainly eaten locally within the county, whereas the double version has become popular across the country.

Single Gloucester is more crumbly and lighter in texture due to a shorter maturing time. Traditionally, it was considered to be an inferior cheese only used to feed local haymakers.

Double Gloucester tends to be made as a larger, firmer-textured cheese, which is matured for longer and has a deeper, stronger and more savoury flavour. The use of annatto natural vegetable colouring makes it a darker orange colour compared to the pale yellow colour of the single variety. It is not definitively known what single and double actually mean, but the main theories relate to either the milk being skimmed twice to make double or extra cream being added to the milk, or because double is twice the height of the single version.

Double Gloucester is the cheese used at the annual Cooper's Hill Cheese Rolling competition held every spring in the Gloucestershire village of Brockworth.

The creamy texture and sweet/savoury flavour of Double Gloucester requires a thick slice of soft-textured, crusty white bread such as a bloomer or a farmhouse – a thick slice is recommended as this soft bread will squash down a little during cooking. This traditional style of bread provides an ideal texture and flavour match for these cheeses.

Martell's Double Gloucester with Orchard Fruits

Charles Martell has been making cheese at Hunts Court in Dymock, Gloucestershire, for over 40 years, and this was the first cheese he made using milk from his own herd of Old Gloucester cows. He uses either pasteurised or unpasteurised milk, depending on the stockist, and vegetarian rennet. The cheese has a firm, smooth, moist texture with a rich, milky aroma and flavours of mellow butteriness, nuttiness and a slight tanginess.

The soft, creamy texture of the cheese pairs well with the crisp, acidic freshness of the apple and pear. By only grilling and not warming beforehand, the fruit maintains its cool crispness and provides an excellent contrast to the hot melted cheese.

Ingredients

1 thick slice of crusty white bloomer or farmhouse bread

½ eating apple, peeled, cored and thinly sliced

½ pear, peeled, cored and thinly sliced

75g Martell's Double Gloucester cheese, grated

Method

❖ Preheat the grill to medium-high.

❖ Toast the bread on both sides and then place on a small baking tray.

❖ Arrange the apple and pear slices on one side of the toast. Scatter the cheese over the top.

❖ Place under the preheated grill until the cheese has melted and is starting to brown.

•

Other cheeses that can be used in this recipe

Double Gloucesters
Appleby's, Smart's, Double Devonshire

Firm cheeses
Cheddar, Red Leicester

Crumbly cheeses
Lancashire, Cheshire, Wensleydale

Appleby's Double Gloucester with Brussels Sprouts

The Appleby family have been making cheese since 1952 at Hawkstone Abbey Farm in Marchamley, Shropshire. Using unpasteurised cheese from their own herd of Holstein-Friesian cows and vegetarian rennet, they have created their own version of Double Gloucester. Although the ingredients are the same as their iconic Cheshire, this cheese has a subtler flavour and lower acidity. It has a full-bodied, smooth and creamy texture with rich, nutty and buttery flavours.

The unusual pairing with the slight nuttiness of the sprouts makes a tasty combination.

Ingredients

1 teaspoon olive oil

75g Brussels sprouts, thinly sliced

½ small onion, thinly sliced

1 thick slice of crusty white bloomer or farmhouse bread

75g Appleby's Double Gloucester cheese, grated

Method

❖ Preheat the grill to medium-high.

❖ Heat the olive oil in a small frying pan, add the sprouts and onion and fry gently for about 5 minutes or until soft but not browned, stirring occasionally.

❖ Meanwhile, toast the bread on both sides and then place on a small baking tray.

❖ Spoon the fried sprouts and onion onto one side of the toast, then sprinkle the cheese on top.

❖ Place under the preheated grill until the cheese has melted and is starting to brown.

•

Other cheeses that can be used in this recipe

Double Gloucesters
Martell's, Smart's, Double Devonshire

Firm cheeses
Cheddar, Red Leicester

Crumbly cheeses
Lancashire, Cheshire, Wensleydale

Smart's Double Gloucester with Chives and Onion

The Smart family make cheese at Old Ley Court in Churcham, Gloucestershire, using milk from their herd of Gloucester, Holstein-Friesian and Brown Swiss cows. Unpasteurised milk from both the morning and evening milkings is used with vegetarian rennet and the cheese is matured for six months. This is the cheese that is traditionally used for the annual Cooper's Hill cheese-rolling event that takes place in spring every year in Brockworth, Gloucestershire.

Chives and onion make delicious, tangy, sharp partners for the smooth, buttery fruitiness of the cheese.

Ingredients

1 teaspoon olive oil

1 small onion, thinly sliced

1 thick slice of crusty white bloomer or farmhouse bread

75g Smart's Double Gloucester cheese, grated

2 teaspoons snipped fresh chives

Method

❖ Preheat the grill to medium-high.

❖ Heat the olive oil in a small frying pan, add the onion and sauté over a medium heat for about 5 minutes or until lightly browned.

❖ Meanwhile, toast the bread on both sides and then place on a small baking tray.

❖ Spoon the sautéed onion over one side of the toast, then scatter the cheese on top.

❖ Place under the preheated grill until the cheese has melted and is starting to brown.

❖ Sprinkle the snipped chives on top just before serving.

•

Other cheeses that can be used in this recipe

Double Gloucesters
Martell's, Appleby's, Double Devonshire

Firm cheeses
Cheddar, Red Leicester

Crumbly cheeses
Lancashire, Cheshire, Wensleydale

Double Devonshire with Sage

This recipe uses another traditional British cheese style that has been created by Mary Quicke on her family farm near Exeter in Devon. This cheese is Quicke's version of a Double Gloucester and with three months' maturing it retains a smooth moistness and firm texture. They use pasteurised milk from their own herd and vegetarian rennet. Rich, buttery flavours are balanced by a slight tanginess.

Simply paired with aromatic sage leaves, this is an uncomplicated but really tasty recipe.

Ingredients

1 thick slice of crusty white bloomer or farmhouse bread

20g unsalted butter

10 fresh sage leaves

75g Double Devonshire cheese, thinly sliced

Method

❖ Preheat the grill to medium-high.

❖ Toast the bread on both sides and then place on a small baking tray.

❖ Melt the butter in a small frying pan, add the sage leaves and fry over a low heat for about 30 seconds or until slightly crispy but not browned. Spoon onto one side of the toast. Lay the cheese slices over the sage.

❖ Place under the preheated grill until the cheese has melted and is starting to brown.

•

Other cheeses that can be used in this recipe

Double Gloucesters
Martell's, Appleby's, Smart's

Firm cheeses
Cheddar, Red Leicester

Crumbly cheeses
Lancashire, Cheshire, Wensleydale

LANCASHIRE

Lancashire is one of the traditional hard territorial cheeses of England made in the northern county of Lancashire. It is made in three distinct and different styles, two of which are traditional and one more modern.

Creamy is a young style that historically was made by farmers' wives using surplus milk. Most small farms only produced limited quantities of milk, which wasn't sufficient to make cheese. As a result, the milk was curdled each day and kept for 2–3 days until there was enough curd to make cheese. This is the only British cheese that is made using curd from several days, each being of differing maturity, which are then blended. It is this method that gives Creamy Lancashire its distinctive character. Matured for 1–3 months, the finished cheese has a creamy, almost fluffy texture, which is exceptionally good for grilling, as it doesn't become stringy when melted.

Tasty is made by the same method as creamy but is matured for much longer – at least six months. This longer maturation allows a stronger, nutty-type flavour to develop.

Crumbly is a newer style of Lancashire developed in the 1950s and is often made outside of the traditional county. Made using the milk from a single day's milking and only matured for 6–8 weeks, it has a higher acidity than the other styles and a fresh, crumbly texture and lighter flavour. In many ways, it resembles other territorial cheeses such as

Wensleydale and Cheshire. Crumbly is the style usually sold as own-brand in many supermarkets and it's rarely made in Lancashire and therefore is less traditional. There is one crumbly style in this section of the book and that is made in the county.

Lancashire cheese, like many of the traditional hard cheeses of Britain, pairs best with a thick slice of traditional farmhouse or bloomer bread – a thick slice is recommended as the bread is soft and will squash down a little during cooking. The creamy, crumbly texture and milky flavour of the cheese match with the creamy, soft texture and firm crust of this traditional white bread.

Mrs Kirkham's Lancashire with Beetroot

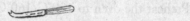

The Kirkham family have been making cheese for three generations at Beesley Farm in Goosnargh, Lancashire, and are now the only makers of tasty, raw milk farmhouse Lancashire cheese. The recipe, using unpasteurised milk from their own herd of Holstein-Friesian cows and traditional rennet, has remained unchanged for 40 years. The Kirkham family describe the texture as a 'buttery crumble' and it has a mixture of tangy, milky and earthy flavours with a hint of fruitiness.

The tanginess of the cheese pairs beautifully with the sweetness of the beetroot, and with them both having earthy flavours, they work together very well.

Ingredients

1 small raw beetroot

1 thick slice of crusty white bloomer or farmhouse bread

1 teaspoon fresh thyme leaves (see Tip)

75g Mrs Kirkham's Lancashire cheese, sliced

Method

❖ Preheat the oven to 180°C/160°C fan/gas 4.

❖ Wrap the beetroot in foil and roast in the oven for about 45 minutes or until soft and a sharp knife easily slides through it. Remove from the oven and leave until it is cool enough to handle, then peel and thinly slice it.

❖ Preheat the grill to medium-high. Toast the bread on both sides and then place on a small baking tray.

❖ Arrange the beetroot slices on one side of the toast and sprinkle the thyme leaves over. Lay the cheese slices on top.

❖ Place under the preheated grill until the cheese has melted and is starting to turn light brown in places.

Tip – If you don't have fresh thyme to hand, use ½ teaspoon dried thyme instead.

•

Other cheeses that can be used in this recipe

Lancashires
Grandma Singleton's, Muldoon's Picnic, Mouth Almighty

Crumbly cheeses
Cheshire, Wensleydale

Firm cheeses
Cheddar, Red Leicester, Double Gloucester

Grandma Singleton's Lancashire Macaroni Cheese

The Singleton family have been making cheese at Mill Farm in Longridge, Lancashire, for four generations, since 1934. Their strong Lancashire Tasty is named after the founder. Using pasteurised milk from local Bowland farms and vegetarian rennet, the cheese is aged for a minimum of 10 months to develop a soft, crumbly texture. It is generally believed to be the strongest of the Lancashire cheeses with a mouthwatering tanginess.

In this recipe, I have used it to make a macaroni cheese that works perfectly as a cheese on toast dish.

Ingredients

50g dried macaroni

2 tablespoons crème fraîche

50g Grandma Singleton's Lancashire cheese, grated

1 thick slice of crusty white bloomer or farmhouse bread

Method

❖ Add the macaroni to a pan of boiling water and cook according to the packet instructions, then drain and return to the pan.

❖ Stir in the crème fraîche until mixed in, then add the cheese, stirring until it is smooth and thick.

❖ Meanwhile, preheat the grill to medium-high. Toast the bread on both sides and then place on a small baking tray.

❖ Spread the macaroni cheese onto one side of the toast.

❖ Place under the preheated grill until the topping is bubbling and starting to turn light brown in places.

•

Other cheeses that can be used in this recipe

Lancashires
Mrs Kirkham's, Muldoon's Picnic, Mouth Almighty

Crumbly cheeses
Cheshire, Wensleydale

Firm cheeses
Cheddar, Red Leicester, Double Gloucester

Muldoon's Picnic with Black Pudding

Saddleworth Cheese Company was formed by Coronation Street actor Sean Wilson in 2009 to make and promote traditional Lancashire cheeses. Using pasteurised milk sourced from the Trough of Bowland in Lancashire and vegetarian rennet, he makes a range of cheeses, with Muldoon's Picnic being his version of Lancashire crumbly. Not surprisingly, the texture is crumbly but retains a pleasing level of moistness. The flavour is milky with a refreshing acidity and bite.

Pairing it with another of Lancashire's traditional foods, black pudding, makes for a delicious match, with the tangy acidity of the cheese working with the richness and sweetness of the black pudding.

Ingredients

75g uncooked black pudding, skin removed and crumbled (see Tip)

1 thick slice of crusty white bloomer or farmhouse bread

75g Muldoon's Picnic cheese, grated

Method

❖ Preheat the grill to medium-high.

❖ Cook the black pudding in a small, dry, non-stick frying pan over a medium heat for about 5 minutes or until it starts to brown slightly, breaking it into crumbs with a wooden spoon as it cooks.

❖ Meanwhile, toast the bread on both sides and then place on a small baking tray.

❖ Spoon the black pudding over one side of the toast, then scatter the cheese on top.

❖ Place under the preheated grill until the cheese has melted and is starting to turn light brown in places.

Tip – Haggis is a good substitute for the black pudding.

•

Other cheeses that can be used in this recipe

Lancashires
Mrs Kirkham's, Grandma Singleton's, Mouth Almighty

Crumbly cheeses
Cheshire, Wensleydale

Firm cheeses
Cheddar, Red Leicester, Double Gloucester

Mouth Almighty with Apple, Raisins and Cinnamon

Former soap opera star, Sean Wilson, of Saddleworth Cheese Company, makes and promotes a range of traditional Lancashire cheeses, including this version, Mouth Almighty. To maintain tradition, he sources pasteurised milk from herds that graze in the Trough of Bowland in Lancashire, to which vegetarian rennet is added. An older style, it is traditional Lancashire Creamy that has been aged for a longer time to develop stronger and sharper flavours. After maturing for anything between 3–12 months, the full flavour has developed beyond its 'Creamy' start in life. It has a creamy, firm texture and a strong tanginess, followed by a rich nuttiness.

Here, the mixture of apple, raisins and cinnamon provides a sweet, spicy contrast to the strong tang of the cheese.

Ingredients

20g unsalted butter

25g raisins

1 teaspoon light soft brown sugar

1 teaspoon ground cinnamon (see Tip)

1 small eating apple, peeled, cored and thinly sliced

1 thick slice of crusty white bloomer or farmhouse bread

75g Mouth Almighty cheese, grated

Method

❖ Preheat the grill to medium-high.

❖ Melt the butter in a small frying pan, then stir in the raisins, sugar and cinnamon. Add the apple slices and cook over a medium heat for about 5 minutes or until they are tender but still retaining their shape, stirring once or twice.

❖ Meanwhile, toast the bread on both sides and then place on a small baking tray.

❖ Pour the apple mixture onto one side of the toast, then scatter the cheese over the top.

❖ Place under the preheated grill until the cheese has melted and is starting to turn light brown in places.

Tip – Swap the cinnamon for freshly grated or ground nutmeg for a tasty flavour variation.

•

Other cheeses that can be used in this recipe

Lancashires
Mrs Kirkham's, Grandma Singleton's, Muldoon's Picnic

Crumbly cheeses
Cheshire, Wensleydale

Firm cheeses
Cheddar, Red Leicester, Double Gloucester

CHESHIRE

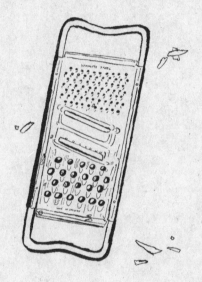

Cheshire cheese is first mentioned in various documents and books during the late sixteenth century with quotes such as 'Cheshire cheese is more agreeable and better relished than those of other parts of the kingdom'.

By 1623, there is the first recorded example of Cheshire cheese being shipped to London by road, although it was a generic term for any cheese made in the county and would most probably have been a hard, aged cheese, not like today's style. 1650 saw the first Cheshire cheese being shipped to London by boat as a result of an outbreak of cattle disease in Suffolk, which had previously been the source of cheese being shipped for the Royal Navy. Cheshire cheese commanded a higher price but proved to be very popular nevertheless; however by the late seventeenth century, demand had reduced due to the loss of many ships during the war with France. The early eighteenth century saw the end of the war and trade for Cheshire cheese again increasing, with London as the major market, and by the middle of the century saw the Royal Navy order that only Cheshire and Gloucester cheese would be used. During this period, the styles of Cheshire cheeses varied immensely but were usually hard and aged to withstand the rigours of transport to London, but by the end of the nineteenth century, a younger, fresher, crumbly style had developed, similar to today's cheese.

Modern-day Cheshire is firm and dense with a moist, crumbly texture and a mildly salty taste. This flavour is as a result of the cows grazing on grass that grows on the salty soil of the Cheshire Plain. The cheese comes in three different styles, with the original being white in colour.

Red Cheshire is coloured with annatto natural vegetable colouring, and it was originally developed in North Wales and sold to travellers en route to Holyhead. Such was the popularity of this cheese that people thought that all Cheshire was orange and many cheesemakers started dying their white cheese to satisfy demand.

Blue Cheshire has blue veins like many other English cheeses and became popular in Georgian London. It has now been revived by some cheesemakers following its decline late last century.

Although Cheshire is similar in texture to other hard British territorial cheeses, the additional saltiness lends it to pairing with a contrasting sweeter style of bread. The flavour of rye or granary bread is generally too strong, but wholemeal bread provides the ideal level of sweetness.

Appleby's Cheshire with Apricots

At the Appleby family's Hawkstone Abbey Farm in Shropshire, their own herd of Holstein-Friesian cows graze on the salty pastures of the Cheshire Plain. The saltiness in the grass imparts a salty flavour to the unpasteurised milk to which vegetarian rennet is added. This is the only unpasteurised clothbound Cheshire made in England today. Coloured with annatto natural vegetable colouring, this orange cheese has a crumbly but moist texture. It has a clean, zesty flavour, almost citrus-like, with salty and savoury herby notes and a refreshing acidity and bite.

The combination of salty cheese with sweet tangy apricots is truly wonderful on the slightly sweet wholemeal bread.

Ingredients

2 fresh ripe apricots, halved and stoned (see Tip)

1 medium slice of wholemeal bread

75g Appleby's Cheshire cheese, grated

Method

❖ Preheat the oven to 180°C/160°C fan/gas 4.

❖ Place the apricots, cut-sides up, on a small baking tray and bake in the oven for about 5 minutes, until softened. Remove from the oven and transfer to a plate.

❖ Toast the bread on both sides and then place on the same small baking tray.

❖ Sprinkle the cheese over one side of the toast. Arrange the apricot halves, cut-sides down, on top of the cheese.

❖ Place under the medium-hot grill until the cheese has melted and the cheese and apricots have started to brown.

Tip – A ripe peach or nectarine is an ideal alternative to the apricots.

•

Other cheeses that can be used in this recipe

Cheshires
Mrs Bourne's, Joseph Heler, Belton Farm

Crumbly cheeses
Lancashire, Wensleydale

Mrs Bourne's Mature Cheshire with Roast Broccoli

The Bourne family have been hand-making Cheshire since 1750, moving to their current location at Bank Farm in Malpas, Cheshire, in 1930. They make a number of different Cheshires, but their mature Cheshire is used in this recipe due to the extra bite and tanginess. Made using pasteurised milk from their own herd of Holstein-Friesian cows and using vegetarian rennet, this crumbly but moist cheese is coloured orange with annatto natural vegetable colouring. The flavour is stronger and tangier than most Cheshires and works well with the natural sweetness of the broccoli in this recipe.

Ingredients

4 broccoli florets, broken into small pieces (see Tip)

2 teaspoons olive oil

a pinch of freshly ground black pepper

1 medium slice of wholemeal bread

75g Mrs Bourne's Mature Cheshire cheese, grated

Method

❖ Preheat the oven to 180°C/160°C fan/gas 4.

❖ Toss the broccoli in the olive oil to coat, place on a small baking tray, then sprinkle over the black pepper. Roast in the oven for about 15 minutes or until lightly browned. Remove from the oven and transfer to a plate.

❖ Preheat the grill to medium-high. Toast the bread on both sides and then place on the same small baking tray.

❖ Arrange the broccoli on one side of the toast. Scatter the cheese over the top.

❖ Place under the preheated grill until the cheese has melted and is starting to brown.

Tip – Tenderstem broccoli also works well in this recipe.

•

Other cheeses that can be used in this recipe

Cheshires
Appleby's, Joseph Heler, Belton Farm

Crumbly cheeses
Lancashire, Wensleydale

Joseph Heler Cheshire with Piccalilli

Joseph Heler have been making traditional Cheshire cheese at Laurels Farm, Nantwich, Cheshire, since 1957, following a 100-year-old family tradition of cheesemaking. They use pasteurised milk from their own and local farms, all located on the Cheshire salt plain, which imparts a natural saltiness to the cheese, along with vegetarian rennet. The pure white cheese has a delicate and crumbly texture, with young, fresh, milky flavours and a zesty citrus finish.

Pairing this salty cheese with tangy, fruity piccalilli creates an uncomplicated but tasty combination served on wholemeal toast.

Ingredients

1 medium slice of wholemeal bread

1 tablespoon piccalilli

75g Joseph Heler Cheshire cheese, grated

Method

❖ Preheat the grill to medium-high.

❖ Toast the bread on both sides and then place on a small baking tray.

❖ Spread the piccalilli on one side of the toast. Scatter the cheese over the top.

❖ Place under the preheated grill until the cheese has melted and is starting to brown.

Other cheeses that can be used in this recipe

Cheshires
Appleby's, Mrs Bourne's, Belton Farm

Crumbly cheeses
Lancashire, Wensleydale

Belton Farm White Cheshire with Mincemeat

This Cheshire cheese is made at the Beckett family's farm, Belton Farm, in Whitchurch, Shropshire. The salty soil of the Cheshire Plain extends as far south as the Shropshire hills and this provides a natural saltiness in the grass that the cows graze upon. The cheese is made using pasteurised milk from local farms with vegetarian rennet, and the salty flavour comes through in the milk and subsequently into the cheese. Belton Farm makes a white and an annatto-coloured orange Cheshire, but the white is recommended for this recipe due to its light, crumbly texture and milky, delicate, salty flavour and slightly citrus tang.

The salty cheese is combined with sweet mincemeat in this simple but delicious pairing.

Ingredients

1 medium slice of wholemeal bread

50g mincemeat (see Tip)

75g Belton Farm White Cheshire cheese, grated

Method

- ❖ Preheat the grill to medium-high.

- ❖ Toast the bread on both sides and then place on a small baking tray.

- ❖ Spread the mincemeat on one side of the toast. Scatter the cheese over the top.

- ❖ Place under the preheated grill until the cheese has melted and is starting to turn light brown in places.

Tip – If you don't have any mincemeat, try using mixed dried fruit instead.

•

Other cheeses that can be used in this recipe

Cheshires
Appleby's, Mrs Bourne's, Joseph Heler

Crumbly cheeses
Lancashire, Wensleydale

WENSLEYDALE

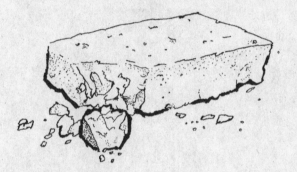

Wensleydale started its life as a blue cheese and it wasn't until 1938 that any record was found for 'white Wensleydale', as we know it today. The original Wensleydale was made by French Cistercian monks who had settled in this area of North Yorkshire in the mid-twelfth century, firstly at a monastery in Fors and later at Jervaulx Abbey. They had brought with them a recipe for a blue sheep's cheese, similar to Roquefort. During the fourteenth century they started using cow's milk instead, until 1540 when the dissolution of the monasteries saw the end of the monks in the area, but local farmers had by this time started copying the monks' cheese and so it continued to be produced locally. This continued until the Second World War, when all milk was used to make 'Government Cheddar', then when rationing ended in 1954, traditional Wensleydale cheesemaking had virtually died out in many farms.

The next key landmark was in the 1930s when Kit Calvert formed a farmers' cooperative at the Wensleydale Creamery in Hawes, and effectively saved traditional Wensleydale-making from extinction. By the 1930s, the production of the traditional blue Wensleydale had died out and only the newer white version was being made. In recent years, however, blue Wensleydale has started to be made again by some cheesemakers. The Milk Marketing Board bought the creamery in the 1960s and they in turn closed it in the early

1990s, but within a few months a management buyout had rescued it and traditional Wensleydale-making has carried on there ever since.

The Wensleydale Creamery in Hawes is the only cheese-maker able to use the name Real Yorkshire Wensleydale; however, the other cheeses in this section are excellent examples of traditionally made Wensleydale-style cheeses but are made using different recipes outside of the historic area of Wensleydale.

Despite being a relatively mild cheese compared to some other styles, Wensleydale exhibits a whole range of flavours, from buttery and creamy through to citrus and savoury. In order to let the flavours shine through, the creamy and crusty texture and flavour of a thick slice of bloomer or farmhouse bread is perfect – a thick slice is recommended as the soft-textured bread will squash down a little during cooking.

Richard III Wensleydale with Cranberries and Walnuts

This traditional Wensleydale was created in the early 1990s by Suzanne Stirke of Fortmayne Dairy in North Yorkshire, when she found an old recipe of her grandmother's in her attic. Later the recipe was passed to Sandhams Dairy where it is still made today. The cheese is made more slowly and is less crumbly and less acidic than most Wensleydales. Made with pasteurised milk and vegetarian rennet, and bound in muslin during maturation, the texture is moist and creamy. The flavour is mild, slightly lemony and becomes lightly honeyed as it ages.

Sweet, tangy cranberries and the toasty flavour of walnuts pair well with the freshness of the cheese in this recipe.

Ingredients

50g walnut pieces

1 teaspoon ground cinnamon

2 teaspoons olive oil

1 thick slice of crusty white bloomer or farmhouse bread

50g dried cranberries

75g Richard III Wensleydale cheese

Method

❖ Preheat the oven to 180°C/160°C fan/gas 4.

❖ Mix the walnuts, cinnamon and olive oil together and place on a small baking tray, then roast in the oven for 5–8 minutes, stirring the mixture every few minutes until the nuts have darkened slightly and have a toasty aroma. Remove from the oven and transfer to a plate.

❖ Meanwhile, preheat the grill to medium-high. Toast the bread on both sides and then place on the same small baking tray.

❖ Scatter the walnut mixture over one side of the toast. Place the cranberries in amongst the walnuts, then crumble the cheese over the top.

❖ Place under the preheated grill until the cheese has melted and is starting to turn light brown in places.

•

Other cheeses that can be used in this recipe

Wensleydales
Real Yorkshire, Whin Yeats Fellstone, Kit Calvert

Crumbly cheeses
Lancashire, Cheshire

Real Yorkshire Wensleydale with Crystallised Ginger

Wensleydale Creamery has been making cheese in Hawes, North Yorkshire, for over 100 years and is currently run by a management team after a buyout in 1992. They source pasteurised milk from small local farms and now hold a Protected Geographical Indication (PGI) for Yorkshire Wensleydale to assure authenticity. They use the traditional way of making real Wensleydale, using traditional rennet, resulting in a less crumbly texture than many imitators. It is a delicate cheese, initially slightly sour, with a honeyed and sweet aftertaste.

The cheese's natural sweet and sourness pairs superbly with the sweet tanginess of crystallised ginger – an unusual but delicious pairing.

Ingredients

1 thick slice of crusty white bloomer or farmhouse bread

50g crystallised ginger, chopped

75g Real Yorkshire Wensleydale cheese, crumbled

Method

❖ Preheat the grill to medium-high.

❖ Toast the bread on both sides and then place on a small baking tray.

❖ Sprinkle the crystallised ginger on one side of the toast. Scatter the cheese over the top.

❖ Place under the preheated grill until the cheese has melted and is starting to turn light brown in places.

Other cheeses that can be used in this recipe

Wensleydales
Richard III, Whin Yeats Fellstone, Kit Calvert

Crumbly cheeses
Lancashire, Cheshire

Whin Yeats Fellstone with Bacon and Mustard

Tom and Clare Noblet have been making a Wensleydale-style cheese at their Hutton Roof dairy near Carnforth, Cumbria, since 2014 when falling milk prices meant they had to find a way of ensuring the future of their farm. They use unpasteurised milk from their own herd of Holstein-Friesians and vegetarian rennet to make this traditional Wensleydale-style cheese. Matured for three months, the cheese is delightfully moist and smooth compared to some more crumbly styles and the flavours are milky, yogurty and buttery with a hint of mushroom.

The buttery flavour of the cheese pairs beautifully with the salty tanginess of bacon and mustard in this recipe.

Ingredients

2 rashers unsmoked back bacon, diced

1 thick slice of crusty white bloomer or farmhouse bread

½ teaspoon English mustard

75g Whin Yeats Fellstone cheese, crumbled

1 spring onion, chopped

Method

❖ Preheat the grill to medium-high.

❖ Cook the bacon in a small, dry, non-stick frying pan over a medium heat for about 5 minutes or until cooked but not browned, stirring occasionally.

❖ Meanwhile, toast the bread on both sides and then place on a small baking tray.

❖ Spread the mustard over one side of the toast. Place the bacon on top.

❖ Mix together the cheese and spring onion and scatter over the bacon.

❖ Place under the preheated grill until the cheese has melted and is starting to turn light brown in places.

•

Other cheeses that can be used in this recipe

Wensleydales
Richard III, Real Yorkshire, Kit Calvert

Crumbly cheeses
Lancashire, Cheshire

Kit Calvert 'Old Style' Wensleydale with Rhubarb

This cheese is named in honour of a man named Kit Calvert who saved Wensleydale Creamery from closure back in 1935. The creamery has been making cheese in Hawes, North Yorkshire, for over 100 years. They source pasteurised milk from small local farms and now hold a Protected Geographical Indication (PGI) for Yorkshire Wensleydale to assure authenticity. It is made in the old-fashioned way and has a clean, fresh taste and creamy citrus flavours.

The tangy bite of another Yorkshire speciality, rhubarb, tempered by the sweetness of the honey, pairs well with this creamy, buttery cheese.

Ingredients

1 stick/stem rhubarb, cut into 5cm lengths

1 teaspoon olive oil

2 teaspoons runny honey

1 teaspoon fresh thyme leaves

1 thick slice of crusty white bloomer or farmhouse bread

75g Kit Calvert 'Old Style' Wensleydale cheese

Method

❖ Preheat the oven to 180°C/160°C fan/gas 4.

❖ Place the rhubarb in an ovenproof dish with the olive oil, honey and thyme leaves and toss to mix. Roast in the oven for about 15 minutes or until the rhubarb is soft but still holding its shape.

❖ Preheat the grill to medium-high. Toast the bread on both sides and then place on a small baking tray.

❖ Arrange the rhubarb on one side of the toast, then pour the juices over. Crumble the cheese on top.

❖ Place under the preheated grill until the cheese has melted and is starting to turn light brown in places.

•

Other cheeses that can be used in this recipe

Wensleydales
Richard III, Yorkshire, Whin Yeats Fellstone

Crumbly cheeses
Lancashire, Cheshire

CAERPHILLY

Caerphilly is a relatively new cheese compared to many of the traditional British territorial cheeses, having first been made in the early nineteenth century as a way for farmers to use excess milk. Increasing demand meant that soon it was being made with all the milk, not just the remainder.

Originally made on farms around the town of Caerphilly in South Wales, it became very popular with miners, as the cheese could be held by the shaped rind without getting coal dust on the cheese itself. Being a relatively moist cheese, it also kept its texture well in the dry, dusty mines, and the salt content of the cheese helped to replace the salt lost in the physical toil of the hard-working miners.

By the start of the twentieth century, many English cheesemakers, particularly in Somerset, had started making Caerphilly, as it was faster to make than traditional Cheddars and therefore was able to be sold quicker and for a cheaper price, giving financial benefits to both the cheesemakers and the customers.

As with many British cheeses, the outbreak of war in 1939 meant that all milk was used to make Government Cheddar, and Caerphilly production ceased.

The Protected Geographical Indication (PGI) for 'Traditional Welsh Caerphilly/Caerffili' specifies that it must be made on a Welsh farm using Welsh milk. There is only one producer of the PGI cheese, Caws Cenarth, makers of

Golden Cenarth and Perl Wen (which appear elsewhere in the book), but this section uses two of the most popular and easy to obtain traditional Caerphillys, both from Somerset. There are also two recipes made using cheeses based on Caerphilly, both of which share similar characteristics with the original.

Caerphilly is a crumbly cheese with a creamy outer layer and a delicate citrus tanginess with some hints of mushroomy flavours, so the savouriness of sourdough bread provides a perfect accompaniment to the complex flavours in this cheese.

Gorwydd Caerphilly with Smoked Haddock and Apple

Todd Trethowan started making traditional Caerphilly in South Wales but moved to a new dairy at Puxton Court Farm near Weston-super-Mare, Somerset, in 2014, where he continues to make this award-winning cheese with his brother, Maugan, and his wife, Kim. They use unpasteurised milk from a local herd of Holstein-Friesian and Jersey cows and traditional rennet. The cheese has two distinct textures when ripe – creamy, buttery and rich near the rind with a crumbly freshness near the centre. Similarly, the flavours differ with a fresh citrus centre and an earthy mushroom flavour at the edge.

A truly delicious cheese whose complex flavours work superbly with this unusual but delicious pairing of smoked fish and apple.

Ingredients

100g smoked haddock fillet (skin on) (see Tips)

50:50 mixture of milk (of your choice) and water – just enough to cover the haddock

1 medium slice of sourdough bread

½ eating apple, peeled, cored and thinly sliced

75g Gorwydd Caerphilly cheese

Method

❖ Place the haddock in a small saucepan and just cover with the milk and water mix. Bring to a simmer and cook for 2 minutes, then remove from the heat and leave to stand for 5 minutes.

❖ Remove the fish with a slotted spoon and cool a little before peeling off the skin. Discard the cooking liquid (or see Tips).

❖ Preheat the grill to medium-high. Toast the bread on both sides and then place on a small baking tray.

❖ Break the fish into chunks and place on one side of the toast. Arrange the apple slices on top and amongst the fish chunks. Crumble the cheese over the top.

❖ Place under the preheated grill until the cheese has melted and is starting to bubble.

Tips – Smoked cod works well instead of smoked haddock. The leftover fishy milk/water can be used for making a sauce or soup, if you use it on the same day.

•

Other cheeses that can be used in this recipe

Caerphilly-style cheeses
Duckett's, Cornish Yarg, Dirty Vicar

Duckett's Caerphilly with Caramelised Apple

In addition to his well-known Cheddar, Tom Calver and the Westcombe Dairy team in Somerset also make this cheese, which is named after its creator, Chris Duckett, who passed it on to Tom when he retired from cheesemaking. Made using unpasteurised milk from Holstein-Friesian cows and traditional rennet, the cheese is aged for 3–4 months to develop a light, firm, slightly crumbly softness. It has complex flavours of citrus, fresh grass and mushroom.

The fresh citrus flavour of the cheese makes a great pairing with the acidic sweetness of caramelised apples.

Ingredients

25g unsalted butter

1 small eating apple, peeled, cored and thinly sliced

1 tablespoon demerara sugar

1 medium slice of sourdough bread

75g Duckett's Caerphilly cheese, thinly sliced

Method

❖ Melt the butter in a small frying pan, add the apple slices and cook over a medium heat for about 5 minutes or until they turn light golden, stirring occasionally.

❖ Add the sugar and cook for a further 5 minutes, stirring until the apple slices are caramelised and tender.

❖ Meanwhile, preheat the grill to medium-high. Toast the bread on both sides and then place on a small baking tray.

❖ Spoon the caramelised apple slices onto one side of the toast. Lay the cheese slices on top.

❖ Place under the preheated grill until the cheese has melted and is starting to bubble.

•

Other cheeses that can be used in this recipe

Caerphilly-style cheeses
Gorwydd, Cornish Yarg, Dirty Vicar

Cornish Yarg with Asparagus and Poached Egg

Yarg was first made in the early 1980s when Cornish farmer Alan Gray found a seventeenth-century recipe and made the nettle-wrapped cheese and reversed his surname to Yarg. When Catherine Mead bought the company, she built Lynher Dairy near Truro, Cornwall, and continued making this unique cheese. It is made using pasteurised milk from their own herd of Ayrshire cows and vegetarian rennet. Similar to a Caerphilly-style cheese, it has a fresh, creamy texture just under the nettles and a soft crumble at the centre. It has a complex flavour starting with a citrus freshness at the centre, maturing to a creamier butteriness at the edges.

Asparagus and a soft poached egg make a perfect pairing for this exciting cheese.

Ingredients

1 teaspoon olive oil

4 asparagus spears, woody ends trimmed off (see Tip)

1 medium slice of sourdough bread

75g Cornish Yarg cheese, sliced

1 medium egg

Method

❖ Heat the olive oil in a frying pan or griddle pan and add the asparagus spears. Cook over a medium heat for about 5 minutes or until the asparagus is lightly charred, turning a few times during cooking.

❖ Meanwhile, preheat the grill to medium-high and bring a small pan of water to a simmer.

❖ Toast the bread on both sides and then place on a small baking tray.

❖ Arrange the asparagus on one side of the toast and lay the cheese slices on top.

❖ Place under the preheated grill until the cheese has melted and is starting to bubble.

❖ Meanwhile, carefully crack the egg into a fine sieve (this allows the watery parts of the white to drain away – it's this watery part that goes stringy during cooking and turns the water cloudy). Gently pour the egg into the pan of simmering water, turn the heat off and leave the egg to poach for 3 minutes (for a perfect soft-yolk egg). Remove with a slotted spoon and drain.

❖ Place the poached egg on top of the bubbling cheese.

Tip – Swap tenderstem broccoli for the asparagus, if you like.

•

Other cheeses that can be used in this recipe

Caerphilly-style cheeses
Gorwydd, Duckett's, Dirty Vicar

Dirty Vicar with Silent Pool Gin-soaked Rhubarb

Made by Michaela and Neil Allam at Norbury Park Farm Cheese Company based at Sherbourne Farm in Albury, Surrey, they are the only commercial cheesemakers in Surrey. Unpasteurised milk from a local herd of British Friesian cows is used with vegetarian rennet. The cheese has a soft, white, Brie-style rind with a Caerphilly-style semi-soft centre.

Flavours of fresh milk, citrus and a slightly mushroom taste make this an ideal cheese to pair with the tangy, boozy rhubarb. The rhubarb is soaked in Silent Pool Gin, which is made in the artisan distillery right next door to the cheese dairy at Sherbourne Farm. After soaking, the gin can be enjoyed as a perfect drink to accompany this recipe.

Ingredients

1 stick/stem rhubarb, cut into 7.5cm lengths

50ml Silent Pool Gin (see Tips)

juice of ½ lemon

1 medium slice of sourdough bread

75g Dirty Vicar cheese, thinly sliced

Method

❖ Place the rhubarb in a shallow dish, add the gin and lemon juice and toss to coat. Cover and set aside to soak for 2 hours.

❖ Transfer the rhubarb and soaking juices to a small pan and cook over a medium heat for about 5 minutes or until it is soft but still holds its shape.

❖ Meanwhile, preheat the grill to medium-high. Toast the bread on both sides and then place on a small baking tray.

❖ Using a slotted spoon, arrange the rhubarb on one side of the toast (see Tips). Lay the cheese slices on top.

❖ Place under the preheated grill until the cheese has melted and is starting to bubble.

Tips – I have used Silent Pool Gin as the distillery is located next door to the cheesemaker, but if you have a favourite gin, try that instead. The leftover gin juices can be used as the basis for a cocktail – why not experiment for yourself?

•

Other cheeses that can be used in this recipe

Caerphilly-style cheeses
Gorwydd, Duckett's, Cornish Yarg

OTHER HARD CHEESES

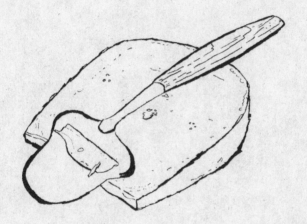

Most traditional British cheeses, as featured in previous pages, would be classified as firm cheeses, with the term 'hard cheeses' being used to describe a more brittle and crumbly style of cheese. The majority of hard cheeses are made in mainland Europe, with famous examples being Parmigiano-Reggiano, Manchego and Gouda. This section deals with the newer styles of hard cheeses made in Britain today. They can be made from cow's, goat's or sheep's milk, but as there are separate sections for the latter two, this section only includes hard cow's milk cheeses.

The two main styles of hard cheeses are pressed uncooked cheeses, which are gently pressed and usually ready for eating within a few weeks, and pressed cooked cheeses, which have the curds heated in the whey before being pressed, generally resulting in a harder, longer-maturing cheese. The longer period of maturing results in full-flavoured cheeses with a distinctive tanginess.

Depending on the exact methods of cheesemaking used, hard cheeses generally have a hard, brittle or grainy texture, and age for several years, some as long as five years. Modern British hard cheeses are usually either based on other European styles or are a hybrid, employing a variety of cheesemaking techniques.

Because this section contains a variety of cheese styles and flavours, the choice of breads varies to suit each cheese.

Ciabatta is a traditional Italian-style accompaniment to the Aubergine Parmigiana recipe, a crusty white is the natural partner for the cheese and Marmite® combo, and the last two recipes particularly suit the tangy flavours of sourdough.

Old Winchester Aubergine Parmigiana

This cheese is made by Mike and Judy Smales of Lyburn Farmhouse Cheesemakers at Lyburn Farm in Landford, Wiltshire, where the family have farmed for 50 years. They use pasteurised milk from their own herd of Holstein-Friesian cows with vegetarian rennet, and using a Gouda recipe, they age the cheese for 16 months. The texture is very hard, almost brittle and has a distinct crystalline crunch. With a tanginess reminiscent of a cross between mature Cheddar and Parmesan, it also has a caramel-like sweetness.

These flavours mean that this is the perfect cheese to pair with this classic Italian-style combination of aubergine, tomato and garlic.

Ingredients

6 teaspoons olive oil

several 5mm-thick slices aubergine (you need enough to cover both halves of the toast)

15cm piece of ciabatta bread, cut in half lengthways

1 garlic clove, halved

2 tablespoons tomato purée

100g Old Winchester cheese, grated

Method

❖ Preheat the grill to medium-high.

❖ Using 4 teaspoons of the olive oil, brush it over each side of the aubergine slices and then place on a small baking tray. Place under the preheated grill and cook for about 3 minutes on each side, until lightly browned, turning once.

❖ Toast the ciabatta halves on both sides and then transfer to a board, cut-sides up.

❖ Rub the garlic halves over the cut sides of the hot toast. Drizzle over the remaining olive oil, then spread the tomato purée on top.

❖ Place the aubergine slices on the toast, then transfer back to the small baking tray. Scatter the cheese over the top.

❖ Place under the preheated grill until the cheese has melted and is starting to turn light brown in places.

•

Other cheeses that can be used in this recipe

Hard cheeses
Sussex Charmer, Doddington, Teifi

Firm cheeses
Cheddar, Red Leicester

Crumbly cheeses
Lancashire, Cheshire, Wensleydale

Sussex Charmer with Marmite®

Bookham and Harrison Farms first made this cheese in 2007 when Rob Bookham, a cheesemaker, and Tim Harrison, a dairy farmer, collaborated to create it. Using pasteurised milk from Tim's herd in Rudgwick, West Sussex, the cheese is actually made at Alvis Bros at Lye Cross Farm, Somerset, using vegetarian rennet. The name 'Charmer' comes from Cheddar and Parmesan to reflect the style of the cheese being similar to a blend of the two. The texture reflects the style of cheese with a firm, moistness combined with a slightly crunchy bite. Flavours combine the creaminess of a farmhouse Cheddar with the tanginess of a Parmesan, and the pairing with Marmite® is truly sublime (if you like Marmite®!)

Ingredients

1 thick slice of crusty white bloomer or farmhouse bread

2 teaspoons Marmite® (see Tip)

75g Sussex Charmer cheese, sliced

Method

❖ Preheat the grill to medium-high.

❖ Toast the bread on both sides and then place on a small baking tray.

❖ Spread the Marmite® on one side of the toast, then lay the cheese slices on top.

❖ Place under the preheated grill until the cheese has melted and is starting to turn light brown in places.

Tip – Marmite® is the top choice for this recipe, but other brands of yeast extract will work just as well.

•

Other cheeses that can be used in this recipe

Hard cheeses
Old Winchester, Doddington, Teifi

Firm cheeses
Cheddar, Red Leicester

Crumbly cheeses
Lancashire, Cheshire, Wensleydale

Doddington with Mushrooms and Garlic

This cheese has been made by the Maxwell family since 1992 at North Doddington Farm in Wooler, Northumberland, using unpasteurised milk from their herd of Holstein-Friesian/Ayrshire-cross cows and traditional rennet. Fully matured for over a year, the cheese is described as being halfway between a Cheddar and a Leicester, with a firm texture and a slightly crystalline crunch. The flavour is rich and salty-sweet with nutty and caramel notes.

The sweet earthiness of the mushrooms and the sweet pungency of the garlic pair well with this full-flavoured cheese.

Ingredients

2 teaspoons olive oil

1 garlic clove, thinly sliced

40g button chestnut mushrooms, thinly sliced

a pinch of dried oregano

1 medium slice of sourdough bread

75g Doddington cheese, grated

Method

❖ Preheat the grill to medium-high.

❖ Heat the olive oil in a small frying pan, add the garlic and mushrooms and sauté over a medium heat for about 5 minutes or until softened and lightly browned. Stir in the oregano.

❖ Meanwhile, toast the bread on both sides and then place on a small baking tray.

❖ Spoon the fried mushrooms and garlic onto one side of the toast, then scatter the cheese on top.

❖ Place under the preheated grill until the cheese has melted and is starting to turn light brown in places.

•

Other cheeses that can be used in this recipe

Hard cheeses
Old Winchester, Sussex Charmer, Teifi

Firm cheeses
Cheddar, Red Leicester

Crumbly cheeses
Lancashire, Cheshire, Wensleydale

Teifi with Chargrilled Artichokes

John Savage-Onstwedder and Paula van Werkhoven moved from The Netherlands to Wales in 1982 and have been making cheese at Caws Teifi Cheese on Glynhynod Farm in Llanduysul, Ceredigion, ever since. They brought a traditional Gouda recipe with them and started making Teifi cheese using locally sourced, organic unpasteurised milk and vegetarian rennet. The cheese has a dense, smooth and creamy texture with a mellow, slightly sweet flavour that becomes deeper and richer as it matures.

The almost caramel-like sweetness of the Teifi and the natural sweetness of the chargrilled artichokes pair well with the savouriness of the sourdough in this recipe.

Ingredients

1 medium slice of sourdough bread

50g (drained weight) chargrilled artichokes in oil (from a jar), chopped

1 teaspoon chopped fresh parsley

75g Teifi cheese, thinly sliced

Method

❖ Preheat the oven to 180°C/160°C fan/gas 4.

❖ Toast the bread on both sides and then place on a
small baking tray.

❖ Arrange the artichokes on one side of the toast and
drizzle over a little oil from the jar. Sprinkle the parsley
over. Top with the cheese slices.

❖ Warm through in the oven for a few minutes, then
transfer under the medium-hot grill until the cheese
has melted and is starting to turn light brown in places.

Other cheeses that can be used in this recipe

Hard cheeses
Old Winchester, Sussex Charmer, Doddington

Firm cheeses
Cheddar, Red Leicester

Crumbly cheeses
Lancashire, Cheshire, Wensleydale

ALPINE-STYLE CHEESES

Alpine-style cheeses are usually categorised as either firm or hard cheeses, but have a very distinctive style, texture and flavour. They are sometimes also referred to as mountain cheeses, or in some countries as Swiss cheese, irrespective of where they come from. Cheeses traditionally made in alpine regions are influenced by two key local factors. Firstly, the variety of grass and plants that the cows graze on add to the complex flavours of the cheeses. Secondly, the use of transhumance grazing techniques, whereby cows move between valley meadows and lush mountain pastures, depending on the season, to ensure they are eating the freshest, greenest grass all the time. Clearly this is not an option in Britain, so the making of alpine-style cheeses comes down to the selection of what milk to use and the cheesemaking techniques to produce the traditional nutty, slightly sweet, supple-textured cheese.

One of the key parts of the cheesemaking process that is used to make these cheeses is the handling of the curd after it has been separated from the whey. The curd is cut into smaller pieces than with many other cheeses, and these are then heated to a high temperature for a short period. These processes, along with the use of Swiss starter cultures, are the elements that give alpine-style cheeses their distinctive flavour and texture. The cheeses used in the recipes in this section are similar to alpine-style cheeses in terms of flavour and texture but are not necessarily made in the same way due to geographical constraints.

The sweet, nutty flavours of these cheeses lend themselves perfectly to the nuttiness of spelt bread, resulting in a perfect pairing. The only exception is the recipe made with Kilcreen cheese, where the addition of squash and cider adds a fruity sweetness that works better with the savoury flavours of soda bread.

Ogleshield New York Deli-style

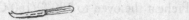

Made by Jamie Montgomery and the team at Manor Farm in North Cadbury, Somerset, who also make the iconic Montgomery's Cheddar featured earlier in the book. This cheese is made using pasteurised rich and creamy milk from Jamie's own herd of Jersey cows. Previously he had only sold it for drinking as the high butterfat content makes it difficult to make a hard cheese. Using traditional rennet, the cheese was originally called 'Shield' and it was only when William Oglethorpe of Neal's Yard Dairy tried rind-washing the cheese to produce a springy-textured, alpine-style cheese, that his name was used to rebrand the cheese.

The rich, creamy and complex flavour and excellent melting characteristic make this a perfect cheese for this classic deli combination, modified to make a wonderful cheese on toast.

Ingredients

1 medium slice of spelt bread

2 teaspoons French mustard

50g pastrami, thinly sliced

50g (drained weight) pickled gherkins or cornichons, halved lengthways

75g Ogleshield cheese, sliced

Method

❖ Preheat the oven to 180°C/160°C fan/gas 4.

❖ Toast the bread on both sides and then place on a small baking tray.

❖ Spread the mustard on one side of the toast. Lay the pastrami over the top.

❖ Arrange the gherkins/cornichons over the pastrami. Lay the cheese slices on top.

❖ Warm through in the oven for a few minutes, then transfer under the medium-hot grill until the cheese is bubbling and starting to brown.

•

Other cheeses that can be used in this recipe

Alpine-style cheeses
Mayfield, Morn Dew, Kilcreen

Mayfield Raclette-style

Mayfield is made by Arthur Alsop and Nic Walker of Alsop and Walker at Coles Hill Barns in Five Ashes, East Sussex, using pasteurised cow's milk from local farms with vegetarian rennet. Sometimes referred to as Mayfield Swiss, its roots are obvious. The semi-hard texture with natural holes (known as eyes) is based on an alpine-style cheese and the creamy, nutty flavours that develop through six months of maturation make this an ideal cheese for melting.

The creamy, sweet, nutty flavours work well with the slightly sweet spelt and contrast beautifully with the traditional raclette accompaniments of pickled baby silverskin onions, cornichons, potatoes and salami. Be warned, this is a filling (but very delicious) dish!

Ingredients

75g baby new potatoes, cut into 5mm-thick slices

1 medium slice of spelt bread

1 teaspoon French mustard

50g salami, thinly sliced

50g (drained weight) pickled silverskin onions, halved

50g (drained weight) pickled gherkins or cornichons, halved lengthways

75g Mayfield cheese, sliced

Method

❖ Preheat the oven to 180°C/160°C fan/gas 4.

❖ Cook the potato slices in a pan of boiling water for about 15 minutes or until soft when pierced with a sharp knife but still retaining their shape. Drain and set aside.

❖ Preheat the grill to medium-high. Toast the bread on both sides and then place on a small baking tray.

❖ Spread the mustard on one side of the toast. Lay the salami over the mustard.

❖ Arrange the onions, gherkins/cornichons and potato slices on the mustard. Lay the cheese slices over the top.

❖ Warm through in the oven for a few minutes, then transfer under the preheated grill until the cheese is bubbling and starting to brown.

•

Other cheeses that can be used in this recipe

Alpine-style cheeses
Ogleshield, Morn Dew, Kilcreen

Morn Dew with Cinnabar Spiced Rum and Raisins

Morn Dew is made by Roger Longman and the team at White Lake Cheese at Bagborough Farm near Shepton Mallet, Somerset, and is named after a well-known quote from 'Only Fools and Horses'. It has an orange soft and sticky rind with a deep golden centre and a soft, spongy texture. Pasteurised Guernsey cow's milk and vegetarian rennet give it a rich colour, texture and flavour.

Raisins are soaked in Cinnabar Spiced Rum, Britain's only rum made from sugar cane. The rum and raisins create a rich, fruity, spicy and deliciously boozy flavour that pairs beautifully with the delicately sweet, creamy and fruity flavour of the cheese. The sweet nuttiness of the spelt bread provides an additional texture and warm flavour.

Ingredients

75g raisins or mixed dried fruit

50ml Cinnabar Spiced Rum (see Tip)

1 medium slice of spelt bread

60g Morn Dew cheese, sliced

Method

❖ Combine the raisins or dried fruit with the rum in a small bowl. Cover and set aside to soak for at least 2 hours.

❖ Preheat the oven to 180°C/160°C fan/gas 4.

❖ Toast the bread on both sides and then place on a small baking tray.

❖ Spoon the soaked raisins or dried fruit over one side of the toast, allowing the rum to soak in. Lay the cheese slices on top.

❖ Warm through in the oven for a few minutes, then transfer under the medium-hot grill until the cheese is bubbling and starting to brown.

Tip – Cinnabar Spiced Rum is the top pick here, but other spiced rums can be used instead.

•

Other cheeses that can be used in this recipe

Alpine-style cheeses
Ogleshield, Mayfield, Kilcreen

Kilcreen with Butternut Squash

Kilcreen is made by Julie and Kevin Hickey and their team at Dart Mountain Cheese in the village of Park, located in the Sperrin Mountains of County Derry, Northern Ireland. Based on an Emmental recipe, it is made using locally sourced pasteurised milk and traditional rennet. Named after a nearby townland (a Gaelic land division), this semi-hard cheese is matured for four months, developing a slightly sweet, nutty flavour.

This recipe combines the sweet nuttiness of the cheese with the sweetness of the squash, plus a hint of fruitiness from the cider and herbs.

Ingredients

1 medium slice of soda bread

75g Kilcreen cheese, grated

75g butternut squash flesh, grated (see Tip)

1 tablespoon dry cider

1 teaspoon fresh thyme leaves

25g unsalted butter, softened

Method

❖ Preheat the oven to 180°C/160°C fan/gas 4.

❖ Toast the bread on both sides and then place on a small baking tray.

❖ Mix together the cheese, butternut squash, cider, thyme leaves and butter. Thickly spread the cheese mix on one side of the toast.

❖ Warm through in the oven for a few minutes, then transfer under the medium-hot grill until the cheese is bubbling and starting to brown.

Tip – Try using sweet potato flesh instead of the butternut squash.

•

Other cheeses that can be used in this recipe

Alpine-style cheeses
Ogleshield, Mayfield, Morn Dew

WASHED-RIND CHEESES

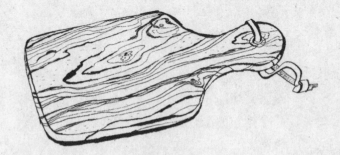

Washed-rind cheeses (sometimes called smear-ripened) are so named because of the process by which the rind is washed or smeared in either brine or alcohol. This washing process encourages the growth of bacteria such as *Brevibacterium linens*, which causes a pink or orange sticky rind to develop with strong, pungent aromas.

The process originated in monasteries in Alsace, France, in the seventh century, where monks created the cheese now known as Munster. Some of the more widely known washed-rind cheeses are also known as Trappist or monastery cheeses. It is thought that the style originated when monks stopped their soft cheese from drying out by washing them in whatever they had available to keep the rind moist and protect the cheese inside. Both soft and hard cheeses can be rind-washed or smear-ripened, but in most cases it is the softer, more pungent ones that are recognised.

The washing is carried out after the cheese has been made and removed from the mould and is holding its shape. The cheeses are then literally washed on a daily basis, usually with salt water but sometimes with alcohol such as brandy, cider or beer. The presence of the wash combined with higher than normal levels of salt in the cheese and a higher than normal pH (lower acidity), encourages the growth of the beneficial bacterium.

As the bacteria grow, they start to make the rind soft and sticky with a pink or orange colour and the pungent, fruity aromas begin to emerge. As the rind flora develops, the flavours and textures inside the cheese also change. The cheese becomes soft and creamy, even oozy in some cases, and the flavours become fruity, yeasty, savoury and sometimes even meaty.

Washed-rind cheeses can be made from cow's, goat's or sheep's milk. Some of the latter two are included in the relevant sections towards the end of the book. This section features cheeses made from cow's milk only, and includes recipes created with washed-rind cheeses made using brine, beer and cider, each of which exhibits different characteristics.

The pungent, fruity and yeasty flavours of these cheeses require a full-flavoured bread with sufficient savoury taste to stand up to the robust characteristics of the cheese. Therefore, the sweet/savoury lactic flavours of soda bread complement washed-rind cheeses perfectly.

Stinking Bishop with Port-poached Pear

Charles Martell created this famous cheese, which came to the world's attention as a result of featuring in a Wallace and Gromit film, using pasteurised milk from his own herd of Old Gloucester cows. The cheese is made using vegetarian rennet and is washed in a perry made from local pears, one variety of which is called Stinking Bishop, hence the name. The rind is pinky orange, soft, sticky and pungent and is wrapped in a small strip of beechwood, with a soft and gooey centre and a pungent, fruity aroma and flavour.

Due to the strong link with pears, I have created this recipe using pears that have been poached in port. The heady, alcoholic flavour of the soft pears matches perfectly with the fruity, strong flavours of the cheese and the sourness of the soda bread.

Ingredients

100ml ruby port

1 cinnamon stick

½ pear, peeled, cored and thinly sliced

1 medium slice of soda bread

75g Stinking Bishop cheese, sliced

Method

❖ Preheat the oven to 180°C/160°C fan/gas 4.

❖ Place the port, cinnamon and 100ml of water in a saucepan and heat until gently simmering. Add the pear slices and poach gently (without a lid) until soft, about 10 minutes.

❖ Preheat the grill to medium-high. Toast the bread on both sides and then place on a small baking tray.

❖ Remove the pears from their cooking liquor using a slotted spoon and drain in a sieve (see Tip), then place on one side of the toast. Lay the cheese slices on top.

❖ Warm through in the oven for a few minutes, then transfer under the preheated grill until the cheese is bubbling and starting to brown.

Tip – Once the pears have been poached, discard the cinnamon stick and use the leftover liquor as the base for a stock or in a casserole.

•

Other cheeses that can be used in this recipe

Washed-rind cow's cheeses
Rollright, Maida Vale, Golden Cenarth

Washed-rind sheep's cheeses
St James

Rollright Tartiflette-style

Made by David Jowett at Manor Farm in Chedworth, Gloucestershire, this soft, washed-rind cheese is inspired by soft, alpine cheeses such as Reblochon. It is made using pasteurised milk from Kings Stone Farm in Little Rollright, Oxfordshire, and traditional rennet. The soft, sticky rind is peach-coloured, mildly pungent and wrapped in a small strip of beechwood, which adds an additional level of flavour as well as holding the cheese in shape. The pale centre is delicate yet full-flavoured with a savoury, yet sweet, buttery flavour.

The cheese's alpine roots make it a perfect base for this tartiflette-inspired recipe, which uses traditional ingredients and creates a tasty and filling dish.

Ingredients

75g baby new potatoes, cut into 5mm-thick slices

50g unsmoked back bacon, diced

1 medium slice of soda bread (see Tip)

50g (drained weight) pickled silverskin onions, halved

50g (drained weight) pickled gherkins or cornichons, halved lengthways

75g Rollright cheese, thinly sliced

Method

❖ Preheat the oven to 180°C/160°C fan/gas 4.

❖ Cook the potato slices in a pan of boiling water for about 15 minutes or until soft when pierced with a sharp knife but still retaining their shape. Drain and set aside.

❖ Meanwhile, cook the bacon in a small, dry, non-stick frying pan over a medium heat for about 5 minutes or until just cooked, stirring occasionally.

❖ Preheat the grill to medium-high. Toast the bread on both sides and then place on a small baking tray.

❖ Arrange the bacon, onions and gherkins/cornichons over one side of the toast. Top with the potato slices. Lay the cheese slices over the top.

❖ Warm through in the oven for a few minutes, then transfer under the preheated grill until the cheese is bubbling and starting to brown.

Tip – Sourdough bread can be used instead of soda bread, if you prefer.

●

Other cheeses that can be used in this recipe

Washed-rind cow's cheeses
Stinking Bishop, Maida Vale, Golden Cenarth

Washed-rind sheep's cheeses
St James

Maida Vale with Pickled Shallots

As well as their famous soft, white-rinded cheeses, Village Maid Cheese in Berkshire also makes this washed-rind cheese using thermised Guernsey milk from a local farm and vegetarian rennet. It is washed in Treason IPA beer from Uprising Brewery in Windsor to create a rind that is pale orange with a sweet, fruity flavour and soft, sticky texture. The rich, soft centre has a tangy, hoppy flavour from the beer-washing and a creamy, buttery texture.

The sharp tanginess of the pickled shallots matches the savoury, hoppy flavour of the cheese, and their sweetness complements the rich, buttery flavour.

Ingredients

100ml red wine vinegar

2 tablespoons caster sugar

1 teaspoon salt

1 banana shallot, thinly sliced into rings (see Tip)

1 medium slice of soda bread

75g Maida Vale cheese, thinly sliced

Method

❖ Put the vinegar, sugar and salt in a small saucepan and heat through, stirring, until the sugar and salt have dissolved. Remove from the heat, add the shallot slices and stir. Transfer the mixture to a bowl, then set aside to pickle for at least an hour, or overnight (in the fridge) if possible. Once they are pickled and ready, drain the shallot slices.

❖ Preheat the oven to 180°C/160°C fan/gas 4.

❖ Toast the bread on both sides and then place on a small baking tray.

❖ Place the pickled shallot slices on one side of the toast. Lay the cheese slices on top.

❖ Warm through in the oven for a few minutes, then transfer under the medium-hot grill until the cheese is bubbling and starting to brown.

Tip – If you don't have time to pickle the shallot, use 1–2 thinly sliced large pickled onions instead.

•

Other cheeses that can be used in this recipe

Washed-rind cow's cheeses
Stinking Bishop, Rollright, Golden Cenarth

Washed-rind sheep's cheeses
St James

Golden Cenarth with Smoked Bacon
and Pickled Onions

Golden Cenarth is made by Carwyn Adams (of Perl Wen fame) in West Wales. It is made using pasteurised milk sourced from local farms and vegetarian rennet. The rind-washing creates a soft cheese with an orange-tinted rind, a springy supple texture and a rich, buttery flavour.

This recipe is based on an alpine tartiflette but uses traditional British smoked bacon and pickled onions instead to create a very tasty dish combining a variety of flavours and textures.

Ingredients

2 rashers unsmoked back bacon, cut into small pieces

1 medium slice of soda bread

2 large pickled onions, drained and thinly sliced

75g Golden Cenarth cheese, thinly sliced

Method

* Preheat the oven to 180°C/160°C fan/gas 4.

* Cook the bacon in a small, dry, non-stick frying pan over a medium heat for about 5 minutes or until just cooked, stirring occasionally.

* Toast the bread on both sides and then place on a small baking tray.

* Spoon the bacon onto one side of the toast. Top with the pickled onions. Lay the cheese slices over the top.

* Warm through in the oven for a few minutes, then transfer under the medium-hot grill until the cheese is bubbling and starting to brown.

•

Other cheeses that can be used in this recipe

Washed-rind cow's cheeses
Stinking Bishop, Rollright, Maida Vale

Washed-rind sheep's cheeses
St James

SMOKED CHEESES

Smoked cheeses are a subset of flavoured cheeses, but for the purposes of this book and due to their popularity, they have a separate section.

The first record of smoked cheese that I have found is the first century Roman poet, Marcus Valerius Martialis (Martial), who was known for his epigrams in which he satirised life in Rome. In one called *Xenia*, he described as follows . . . 'the low lying Velabrum, between the Forum and Forum Boarium . . . it was particularly known for its smoked cheese, a peculiarly Roman taste: that cheese has a kick to it'.

His contemporary, Pliny the Elder, in his notable work, *Naturalis Historia*, is quoted as saying 'Goats also produce a cheese which has been of late held in the highest esteem, its flavour being heightened by smoking it'.

It is believed that the very earliest smoked cheese was made by accident when cheese was exposed to smoke in primitive huts, but very soon it was discovered that the process of exposing cheese to smoke extended its usable life, becoming one of the earliest forms of food preservation. As can be seen in the Roman examples above, it was quickly discovered that the smoke enhanced the flavour of the cheese.

Today, smoking of cheese is carried out solely to add further flavour and complexity to cheese, as well as creating a visually pleasing colour. Traditionally, smoked cheese is achieved through the cold-smoking process whereby the smoke is transferred from the heat source to the smoking area. It is possible to add smoke-like flavours through the use of smoke flavourings or liquid smoke, but traditional cheesemakers will always use cold-smoking.

The intensity of flavour resulting from the smoking of cheese means that a full-flavoured bread is needed, but pairing with smoked foods can be difficult. The rich, nutty flavours of spelt bread complement the smokiness very well in the following recipes.

Quicke's Oak Smoked Cheddar with
Spicy Maple Apple

This recipe features the oak-smoked version of Mary Quicke's award-winning Cheddar from her family farm in Devon. The cheese is made using pasteurised milk and traditional rennet from their own herd and is cloth-wrapped and matured for 9–12 months, before being cold-smoked over oak chips from trees on their estate. The rich, tangy cheese has a smooth, mellow, smoky flavour that is totally natural and tasty without being overpowering.

In this recipe, the cheese is paired with sweet and spicy apples glazed in maple syrup to give an amazing combination of sweet, spicy and smoky flavours.

Ingredients

1 small eating apple, peeled, cored and sliced

2 tablespoons maple syrup

½ teaspoon ground cinnamon

½ teaspoon freshly grated or ground nutmeg

½ teaspoon Dijon mustard (see Tip)

1 medium slice of spelt bread

75g Quicke's Oak Smoked Cheddar cheese, sliced

Method

❖ Preheat the oven to 180°C/160°C fan/gas 4.

❖ Put the apple slices, maple syrup, spices and mustard in a small saucepan and cook over a low heat for about 10 minutes or until the apple slices are soft but still just holding their shape.

❖ Meanwhile, preheat the grill to medium-high. Toast the bread on both sides and then place on a small baking tray.

❖ Pour the apple mixture over one side of the toast. Lay the cheese slices on top.

❖ Warm through in the oven for a few minutes, then transfer under the preheated grill until the cheese is bubbling and starting to brown.

Tip – Any French or mild English mustard can be used in place of the Dijon mustard.

•

Other cheeses that can be used in this recipe

Smoked cheeses
Montgomery's Smoked Cheddar, Dorset Red, Westcombe Smoked Cheddar

Montgomery's Smoked Cheddar with Barbecue Sausage

Known for their famous Cheddar, which appears in the first section of this book, Jamie Montgomery and the team in North Cadbury, Somerset, also produce a smoked version at Manor Farm. Made using unpasteurised milk from their own herd of Holstein-Friesian cows with traditional rennet, the cheeses are naturally smoked to create a full-flavoured smoked cheese. The cheeses are matured for at least 12 months before being cut into large wedges and hand-smoked for 6 hours over oak chips to give a deep, intense, smoky flavour with rich, nutty notes.

Pairing this robust, almost meaty cheese with pork sausages in a barbecue sauce creates a flavour sensation reminiscent of outdoor summer eating.

Ingredients

2 pork sausages

½ onion, finely diced

1 tablespoon barbecue sauce

1 medium slice of spelt bread

75g Montgomery's Smoked Cheddar cheese, sliced

Method

❖ Remove the skins from the sausages and crumble the meat into a dry non-stick frying pan. Add the onion and cook over a medium heat for about 10 minutes or until the sausagemeat is lightly browned, stirring occasionally. Remove from the heat, add the barbecue sauce and stir well.

❖ Meanwhile, preheat the grill to medium-high. Toast the bread on both sides and then place on a small baking tray.

❖ Spoon the sausage mixture onto one side of the toast, then lay the cheese slices on top.

❖ Place under the preheated grill until the cheese is bubbling and starting to brown.

•

Other cheeses that can be used in this recipe

Smoked cheeses
Quicke's Oak Smoked Cheddar, Dorset Red,
Westcombe Smoked Cheddar

Dorset Red with Smoked Ham

Made at Ford Farm Dairy on the Ashley Chase Estate near Dorchester, Dorset, this traditional handmade West Country Farmhouse Cheddar is made using pasteurised milk from local herds and vegetarian rennet. They use a slightly different process to make the cheese using lower temperatures and less stirring to produce a softer, milder cheese, which is coloured using annatto natural vegetable colouring to give a deep orange colour. Cold-smoking over oak chips creates a mellow, smoky flavour whilst maintaining a firm but silky, soft texture.

Pairing the cheese with smoked ham results in a delicious combination for those who like a lot of smoky flavours in one dish.

Ingredients

1 medium slice of spelt bread

75g smoked ham of your choice, sliced

75g Dorset Red cheese, sliced

Method

❖ Preheat the oven to 180°C/160°C fan/gas 4.

❖ Toast the bread on both sides and then place on a small baking tray.

❖ Arrange the smoked ham on one side of the toast. Lay the cheese slices on top.

❖ Warm through in the oven for a few minutes, then transfer under the medium-hot grill until the cheese is bubbling and starting to brown.

Other cheeses that can be used in this recipe

Smoked cheeses
Quicke's Oak Smoked Cheddar, Montgomery's Smoked Cheddar, Westcombe Smoked Cheddar

Westcombe Smoked Cheddar with Beef Jerky and Onion

Tom Calver and the team at Westcombe Dairy in Somerset make this smoked version of their famous Cheddar using unpasteurised milk from their own herd of Holstein-Friesian cows and traditional rennet, before the cheese is aged for at least 12 months in their purpose-built maturing cave, dug into a hillside. After ageing, the cheeses are portioned and then cold-smoked for 12 hours using cherry wood in a converted phone box at the dairy. This longer than usual smoking time and use of cherry wood gives a deep, russet-coloured and richly aromatic cheese with a deep, smoky flavour.

Pairing it with thin strips of beef jerky gives an intense, full-flavoured dish that will satisfy any appetite.

Ingredients

1 teaspoon olive oil

½ small onion, thinly sliced

1 medium slice of spelt bread

50g beef jerky strips (see Tip)

75g Westcombe Smoked Cheddar cheese, sliced

Method

❖ Preheat the oven to 180°C/160°C fan/gas 4.

❖ Heat the olive oil in a small frying pan, add the onion and fry over a medium heat for about 5 minutes or until just starting to brown, stirring occasionally.

❖ Meanwhile, toast the bread on both sides and then place on a small baking tray.

❖ Spoon the fried onion onto one side of the toast, then place the beef jerky over the onion. Lay the cheese slices on top.

❖ Warm through in the oven for a few minutes, then transfer under the medium-hot grill until the cheese is bubbling and starting to brown.

Tip – Swap in strips of biltong for the beef jerky, if you like.

•

Other cheeses that can be used in this recipe

Smoked cheeses
Quicke's Oak Smoked Cheddar, Montgomery's Smoked Cheddar, Dorset Red

FLAVOURED CHEESES

This category includes any cheese that has additional flavours added at any stage of the cheesemaking. Smoked cheeses are normally included in this category but have already been covered in the previous section of the book. Another method of adding extra flavours is known as re-pressing or re-forming, and this is when young cheeses are chopped up, flavours are added and then the cheese is re-pressed into the desired shape, which is often coated in wax after re-pressing. This method is not considered to be traditional or artisan and therefore does not feature in this book, but the two remaining methods of adding flavour feature in this section.

Started in the sixteenth century, Dutch traders returning from the East Indies brought with them new and exotic spices, such as cumin, caraway and peppercorns, which cheesemakers seized upon to add to their cheese. The spices were added to the fresh curds before placing them into moulds, allowing the flavours to merge and integrate into the cheese itself. Cheesemakers still employ these methods today, with cumin and caraway still being used across the world. In Britain, the practice has extended to include fruit, nuts, herbs and garlic.

Rind-flavoured cheeses are created by natural ingredients being wrapped around or pressed into the rind of the young cheeses. Nettles, hops, wild garlic leaves and concentrated grape juice must have all been used for flavouring using this method.

All of the cheeses used in the following recipes have very distinctive flavourings added, otherwise they would be indiscernible compared to the cheese flavour. A strong-tasting bread is therefore required and the savoury tanginess of sourdough is an ideal partner for all these cheeses, with the exception of Sharpham Chive and Garlic where a Mediterranean flavour is called for.

Lyburn Garlic and Nettle with Spinach and Mushrooms

Best known for their iconic Old Winchester cheese, Mike and Judy Smales, of Lyburn Farmhouse Cheesemakers in Wiltshire, have created this distinctively flavoured version of a younger cheese. They use pasteurised milk from their own herd of Holstein-Friesians with vegetarian rennet. This delicious flavoured cheese starts by being made to a Gouda-style recipe, but then has a fascinating blend of garlic, chives, parsley, paprika, ginger, horseradish and nettles added to produce a unique flavour combination.

The addition of spinach and mushrooms to this recipe creates a whole range of tastes in this delicious dish.

Ingredients

20g unsalted butter

2 chestnut mushrooms, thinly sliced

1 medium slice of sourdough bread

12 baby spinach leaves

75g Lyburn Garlic and Nettle cheese, sliced

Method

❖ Preheat the oven to 180°C/160°C fan/gas 4.

❖ Melt the butter in a small frying pan, add the mushrooms and sauté over a medium heat for about 5 minutes or until soft and lightly browned.

❖ Meanwhile, toast the bread on both sides and then place on a small baking tray.

❖ Lay the spinach leaves over one side of the toast. Spoon the mushrooms and any buttery juices over the spinach. Lay the cheese slices on top.

❖ Warm through in the oven for a few minutes, then transfer under the medium-hot grill until the cheese is bubbling and starting to brown.

•

Other cheeses that can be used in this recipe

Flavoured cheeses
Wild Garlic Yarg, Sharpham Chive and Garlic, Fowler's Sage Derby, Quicke's Elderflower, Tornegus, Hereford Hop, Truffler

Wild Garlic Yarg with Wild Mushrooms and Parsley

Made by Catherine Mead and her team at Lynher Dairy near Truro in Cornwall, this is a truly unique cheese. Based on the original Cornish Yarg, featured in an earlier recipe, it is made using pasteurised milk from their own herd of Ayrshire cows and uses vegetarian rennet. The original cheese is wrapped in nettle leaves, but this version uses wild garlic leaves that have been foraged from local woodlands to give a deep green pattern on the cheese. The centre has a fresh, creamy moistness and a slightly sweet, tangy garlic flavour.

This recipe continues the wild foraging theme by pairing the cheese with wild mushrooms, although it's safer to use shop-bought wild mushrooms than foraging for your own.

Ingredients

20g unsalted butter

50g fresh girolle or chanterelle mushrooms, roughly chopped (see Tip)

1 tablespoon finely chopped fresh parsley

1 medium slice of sourdough bread

75g Wild Garlic Yarg cheese, sliced

Method

❖ Preheat the grill to medium-high.

❖ Melt the butter in a small frying pan, add the mushrooms and sauté over a medium heat for about 5 minutes or until soft and lightly browned. Stir in the parsley.

❖ Meanwhile, toast the bread on both sides and then place on a small baking tray.

❖ Spoon the mushrooms and any buttery juices over one side of the toast. Lay the cheese slices on top.

❖ Place under the preheated grill until the cheese has melted and is starting to bubble.

Tip – If you can't find girolle or chanterelle mushrooms, try using other edible fresh wild mushrooms of your choice.

•

Other cheeses that can be used in this recipe

Flavoured cheeses
Lyburn Garlic and Nettle, Sharpham Chive and Garlic, Fowler's Sage Derby, Quicke's Elderflower, Tornegus, Hereford Hop, Truffler

Sharpham Chive and Garlic with
Sun-dried Tomatoes

Based on their original Sharpham Rustic cheese, Greg and Nicky Parsons and the team at Sharpham Estate in Devon have created this flavoured version using unpasteurised Jersey milk and vegetarian rennet. This semi-hard cheese is flavoured with fresh puréed garlic and chives, and the use of Jersey milk gives the cheese a rich, golden colour and a creamy, slightly crumbly texture. The garlic and chives give the cheese a fresh, savoury flavour that combines with the butteriness to give a truly delicious taste sensation.

The addition of sun-dried tomatoes and the use of ciabatta bread give an almost Mediterranean feel to this recipe, and the acidity of the tomatoes complements the rich creaminess of the cheese.

Ingredients

15cm piece of ciabatta bread, cut in half lengthways

50g (drained weight) sun-dried tomatoes in oil (from a jar), roughly chopped

100g Sharpham Chive and Garlic cheese

Method

❖ Preheat the oven to 180°C/160°C fan/gas 4.

❖ Toast the ciabatta halves on both sides and then place on a small baking tray, cut-sides up.

❖ Scatter the sun-dried tomatoes on the cut sides of the toast, then drizzle over a little oil from the jar. Crumble the cheese over the top.

❖ Warm through in the oven for a few minutes, then transfer under the medium-hot grill until the cheese has melted and is starting to bubble.

Other cheeses that can be used in this recipe

Flavoured cheeses
Lyburn Garlic and Nettle, Wild Garlic Yarg, Fowler's Sage Derby, Quicke's Elderflower, Tornegus, Hereford Hop, Truffler

Fowler's Sage Derby with Courgette

Made by Fowler's Forest Dairy who have been making cheese for 14 generations in Earlswood, Warwickshire, this cheese is flavoured with a layer of real sage leaves, unlike the commercially produced versions which use dyes and flavourings. Using pasteurised milk from their own herd of Holstein-Friesian cows and vegetarian rennet, the cheese is made to a traditional Derby recipe, which has a mellow, nutty flavour. A layer of sage runs through the middle of the cheese and is sprinkled on the natural rind to give a fresh, herby flavour.

Here, fresh courgette complements the grassy, herby flavours of the cheese to give a light and refreshing dish.

Ingredients

1 medium slice of sourdough bread

1 small courgette, sliced into thin rounds

75g Fowler's Sage Derby cheese, sliced

Method

❖ Preheat the oven to 180°C/160°C fan/gas 4.

❖ Toast the bread on both sides and then place on a small baking tray.

❖ Arrange the courgette slices over one side of the toast. Lay the cheese slices on top.

❖ Warm through in the oven for a few minutes, then transfer under the medium-hot grill until the cheese has melted and is starting to bubble.

Other cheeses that can be used in this recipe

Flavoured cheeses
Lyburn Garlic and Nettle, Wild Garlic Yarg, Sharpham Chive and Garlic, Quicke's Elderflower, Tornegus, Hereford Hop, Truffler

Quicke's Elderflower with Beetroot and Pine Nuts

Created by Mary Quicke and her team at Home Farm in Devon, this delicately flavoured cheese is made using their young, buttery Cheddar and local elderflowers. The cheese is made using pasteurised milk from their own herd of hybrid Montbeliarde, Scandinavian Red, Holstein-Friesian and Jersey cows with vegetarian rennet. It is matured for only three months to retain the fresh and buttery flavours. Fresh, wild, foraged Devon elderflowers run through the cheese giving a lovely herby flavour that is unique and lingering.

The freshness of the cheese has been paired with the earthy sweetness of beetroot and the nuttiness and crunch of toasted pine nuts to give a delicious combination.

Ingredients

1 small raw beetroot

20g pine nuts (see Tip)

1 medium slice of sourdough bread

75g Quicke's Elderflower cheese, sliced

Method

❖ Preheat the oven to 180°C/160°C fan/gas 4.

❖ Wrap the beetroot in foil and roast in the oven for about 45 minutes or until soft and a sharp knife easily slides through it. Remove from the oven and leave until it is cool enough to handle, then remove the skin by rubbing with kitchen paper and thinly slice the beetroot.

❖ Meanwhile, lightly toast the pine nuts in a small, dry frying pan over a low heat for a few minutes, until lightly browned, shaking the pan to keep them moving (don't leave them unattended as they will burn easily). Remove from the heat and set aside to cool.

❖ Preheat the grill to medium-high. Toast the bread on both sides and then place on a small baking tray.

❖ Arrange the beetroot on one side of the toast and scatter the pine nuts over. Lay the cheese slices on top.

❖ Warm through in the oven for a few minutes, then transfer under the preheated grill until the cheese is bubbling and starting to brown.

Tip – Try using walnut pieces instead of the pine nuts.

●

Other cheeses that can be used in this recipe

Flavoured cheeses
Lyburn Garlic and Nettle, Wild Garlic Yarg, Sharpham Chive and Garlic, Fowler's Sage Derby, Tornegus, Hereford Hop, Truffler

Tornegus with Chilli Jam

Created by James Aldridge, a true legend of English cheesemaking, this deliciously tasty cheese is made by starting with a traditional Caerphilly, made by Duckett's in Somerset, using pasteurised milk and vegetarian rennet. The fresh cheeses are then transferred to Pat Robinson (James's widow) of Eastside Cheese in Godstone, Surrey, where they are washed in brine, wine, lemon verbena and Egyptian mint. This results in a pale orange, sticky rind with a distinct pungency. The centre is semi-hard, silky and smooth with a spicy, boozy flavour.

The pairing with sharp, but not too hot, chilli jam makes for an excellent contrast and the sourdough lends an additional tangy flavour to complete this full-flavoured recipe.

Ingredients

1 medium slice of sourdough bread

25g chilli jam

75g Tornegus cheese, sliced

Method

❖ Preheat the grill to medium-high.

❖ Toast the bread on both sides and then place on a small baking tray.

❖ Spread the chilli jam onto one side of the toast, then lay the cheese slices on top.

❖ Place under the preheated grill until the cheese is bubbling and starting to brown.

Other cheeses that can be used in this recipe

Flavoured cheeses
Lyburn Garlic and Nettle, Wild Garlic Yarg, Sharpham Chive and Garlic, Fowler's Sage Derby, Quicke's Elderflower, Hereford Hop, Truffler

Hereford Hop with Crispy Fried Onion

Charles Martell, of Stinking Bishop fame, makes this unusual and unique cheese at Hunts Court Farm in Gloucestershire, using pasteurised milk from his own herd of Old Gloucester cows and vegetarian rennet. This semi-hard cheese has a crust made from toasted hops, which gives it a rich, toasty flavour. The outside is slightly bitter and crunchy, whilst the inside is mild, buttery and lemony and has a yeasty, beery savouriness.

The sweetness of the fried onion and butter contrasts perfectly with the sourness of the cheese in this tasty recipe.

Ingredients

20g unsalted butter

1 small onion, thinly sliced

1 medium slice of sourdough bread

75g Hereford Hop cheese, sliced

Method

❖ Melt the butter in a small frying pan, add the onion and fry over a medium heat for about 10 minutes, until evenly browned and crispy, stirring regularly.

❖ Meanwhile, preheat the grill to medium-high. Toast the bread on both sides and then place on a small baking tray.

❖ Spoon the crispy fried onion (and any buttery juices) onto one side of the toast. Lay the cheese slices on top.

❖ Place under the preheated grill until the cheese has melted and is starting to bubble.

•

Other cheeses that can be used in this recipe

Flavoured cheeses
Lyburn Garlic and Nettle, Wild Garlic Yarg, Sharpham Chive and Garlic, Fowler's Sage Derby, Quicke's Elderflower, Tornegus, Truffler

Truffler with Toasted Hazelnuts and Honey

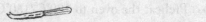

This traditional handmade West Country Farmhouse Cheddar is made at Ford Farm Dairy in Dorset using pasteurised milk from local herds and vegetarian rennet. It is blended with black truffle and mushroom salsa and aromatic black truffle oil. The truffle infuses the Cheddar to create an aroma and a flavour that is strong and heady.

The warm nuttiness of the toasted hazelnuts and the rich sweetness of the honey pair beautifully with the rich truffle flavours of the cheese to create a luxurious combination, contrasting perfectly with the tanginess of the sourdough.

Ingredients

25g blanched whole hazelnuts (see Tip)

1 medium slice of sourdough bread

75g Truffler cheese, sliced

1 tablespoon runny honey

Method

❖ Preheat the oven to 180°C/160°C fan/gas 4.

❖ Place the hazelnuts on a small baking tray. Roast in the oven for about 15 minutes or until they are evenly browned and smell nutty, shaking the tray every 5 minutes. Remove from the oven and cool slightly, then roughly chop.

❖ Preheat the grill to medium-high. Toast the bread on both sides and then place on the same small baking tray.

❖ Arrange the cheese slices on one side of the toast, then press the hazelnuts into the cheese.

❖ Place under the preheated grill until the cheese is bubbling and starting to brown.

❖ Drizzle the honey over the top just before serving.

Tip – Replace the hazelnuts with blanched almonds or pine nuts, if you prefer.

•

Other cheeses that can be used in this recipe

Flavoured cheeses
Lyburn Garlic and Nettle, Wild Garlic Yarg, Sharpham Chive and Garlic, Fowler's Sage Derby, Quicke's Elderflower, Tornegus, Hereford Hop

FETA-STYLE CHEESES

Feta-style cheeses are similar in texture and flavour to those made to the original Greek recipe. The Greek version has Protected Designation of Origin (PDO), covering the use of only sheep's or goat's milk, the cheesemaking method and storage in brine.

The British cheeses in this section cannot use the name 'Feta' nor are they subject to the same conditions. They have been selected for their creamy, crumbly texture and their strong, salty flavour.

Made in Yorkshire, West Sussex, Kent and Somerset, these four cheeses are all slightly different in the way in which they are made and matured. Dry salting, wax coating, brine soaking and preserving in infused olive oil are all different techniques used to make these exciting modern British cheeses.

None of these recipes involve heating or cooking the cheese, as the freshness and saltiness of each of the cheeses make them perfect for serving cold and being paired with delicious complementary ingredients.

The predominant taste that features in all of these Feta-style cheeses is salt, due to its extensive use in their manufacture. The appropriately named sourdough has a sharp sourness that works perfectly with these styles of cheese.

Yorkshire Fettle Greek-style

Yorkshire Fettle is made by Judy Bell and her daughters, Katie and Caroline, at Shepherds Purse Artisan Cheeses in Thirsk, North Yorkshire. Using pasteurised milk from their own herd of sheep and vegetarian rennet, this Feta-style cheese is handmade and hand-salted to create the slightly crumbly texture and piquant, lemony flavour. Each cheese is then hand-waxed to retain the flavour and moist, creamy texture.

This recipe is not cooked but is served in a style similar to a Greek salad on toasted sourdough. It is mouthwateringly fresh and delicious as a summer dish.

Ingredients

1 medium slice of sourdough bread

75g Yorkshire Fettle cheese, crumbled

3cm piece of cucumber, roughly chopped

1 medium tomato, roughly chopped

10 pitted black olives, roughly chopped

2 teaspoons olive oil

1 teaspoon dried oregano

Method

❖ Preheat the grill to medium-high.

❖ Toast the bread on both sides and then place on a plate.

❖ Mix together the cheese, cucumber, tomato and olives in a small bowl. Drizzle over the olive oil and toss to mix. Sprinkle the oregano over the top.

❖ Pile the cheese mixture on top of the toast.

Other cheeses that can be used in this recipe

Feta-style cheeses
Medita, Graceburn, Fetish

Medita with Avocado and Pomegranate Seeds

Medita is made at High Weald Dairy in West Sussex by Mark and Sarah Hardy. Using organic pasteurised milk from their own herd of British Friesland sheep and vegetarian rennet, they produce this Feta-style cheese. Made by the traditional method, it has a creamy texture but crumbles easily. Flavours are sharp and fresh with a citrusy taste and a salty tang.

The creamy sweetness of the avocado and the sharpness of the pomegranate seeds and lime pairs perfectly with the salty creaminess of the cheese. The use of uncooked, fresh ingredients in this recipe makes it deliciously tasty on a warm day.

Ingredients

1 medium slice of sourdough bread

1 medium ripe avocado

1 lime, cut in half

75g Medita cheese, crumbled into chunks

1 tablespoon pomegranate seeds

Method

* Preheat the grill to medium-high.

* Toast the bread on both sides and then place on a plate.

* Remove the skin and stone from the avocado and mash the flesh in a bowl. Squeeze over the juice from half the lime and mix.

* Spread the avocado mix onto the toast, then crumble the cheese on top.

* Sprinkle the pomegranate seeds over the cheese. Squeeze the remaining lime half over the top.

•

Other cheeses that can be used in this recipe

Feta-style cheeses
Yorkshire Fettle, Graceburn, Fetish

Graceburn with Roasted Tomatoes and Olives

Graceburn is made by Dave Holton and Tim Jarvis of Blackwoods Cheese Company at Bore Place in Chiddingstone, Kent, using milk from Common Work Organic Farm on the same estate. The cheese is made from unpasteurised organic cow's milk with traditional rennet and is based on a Persian Fetta, which is creamier and softer than traditional Greek Feta. It comes steeped in extra virgin olive and rapeseed oils with garlic, thyme, bay and pepper.

This recipe combines the Mediterranean aromatic nature of the cheese with roasted tomatoes and olives on toasted sourdough, to produce a tasty combination of aromas and flavours.

Ingredients

75g vine-ripened tomatoes, roughly chopped

25g Kalamata olives, pitted and halved

2 teaspoons olive oil

½ teaspoon freshly ground black pepper

1 medium slice of sourdough bread

75g Graceburn cheese, crumbled into chunks

5 fresh basil leaves, torn into pieces

Method

❖ Preheat the oven to 180°C/160°C fan/gas 4.

❖ Place the tomatoes and olives on a small baking tray. Drizzle over the olive oil, then sprinkle with the black pepper. Roast in the oven for 15 minutes or until the tomatoes are starting to darken around the edges. Remove from the oven and leave to cool completely.

❖ Preheat the grill to medium-high.

❖ Toast the bread on both sides and then place on a plate.

❖ Mix the cooled roasted tomatoes and olives, the cheese and basil in a bowl. Pile the cheesy mixture on top of the toast.

•

Other cheeses that can be used in this recipe

Feta-style cheeses
Yorkshire Fettle, Medita, Fetish

Fetish with Minted Peas

As well as the famous range of goat's milk cheeses, Roger Longman and the team at White Lake Cheese in Somerset have also created this Feta-style cheese using thermised sheep's milk from a local herd and vegetarian rennet. It is a brilliant white colour with a semi-hard, smooth, creamy but crumbly texture. The flavour is tangy, salty and mildly nutty.

The minty freshness of the peas and the sour creaminess of the yogurt provide a great pairing with the cheese in this recipe, which is not cooked and is served on toasted sourdough.

Ingredients

1 medium slice of sourdough bread

50g frozen peas, defrosted at room temperature

1 tablespoon natural yogurt

2 teaspoons chopped fresh mint

finely grated zest and juice of 1 lemon

75g Fetish cheese

1 teaspoon olive oil

Method

❖ Preheat the grill to medium-high.

❖ Toast the bread on both sides and then place on a plate.

❖ Partly crush the defrosted peas in a small bowl with a fork. Add the yogurt, mint and lemon zest and juice and mix.

❖ Spread the pea mixture on one side of the toast. Crumble the cheese on top, then drizzle over the olive oil.

•

Other cheeses that can be used in this recipe

Feta-style cheeses
Yorkshire Fettle, Medita, Graceburn

STILTON-STYLE BLUE CHEESES

Stilton cheese first became well known in the early eighteenth century when it appeared in several books and publications, including one by William Stukeley who wrote in 1722 'Stilton is famous for cheese, which they sell for 12d per pound, and would be thought equal to Parmesan'. Daniel Defoe in 1724 wrote 'We pass'd Stilton, a town famous for cheese, which is call'd our English Parmesan, and is brought to the table with the mites, or maggots round it, so thick, that they bring a spoon with them for you to eat the mites with, as you do the cheese'.

The village of Stilton that Defoe refers to was a staging post on the Great North Road, the main road from London to Yorkshire and Edinburgh. One of the most popular stopping points in the village was the Bell Inn, where the landlord, Cooper Thornhill, sold local produce to travellers, including a blue cheese made in the neighbouring county of Leicestershire. Soon it became known as the blue cheese from Stilton as its fame spread across the country.

Stilton is undoubtedly one of England's greatest cheeses that is much copied throughout the world, but the name Stilton is covered by a Protected Designation of Origin (PDO) stating that it can only be produced in the English counties of Nottinghamshire, Leicestershire and Derbyshire. At the time of writing, only six dairies are licensed to make Stilton cheese (three in Leicestershire, two in Nottinghamshire and one in Derbyshire). Despite many attempts to change the regulations, a cheese made in the village of Stilton cannot be called Stilton because the village is actually in Cambridgeshire.

Sweet, fruity accompaniments, such as figs and dates, pair well with the complex flavours and textures of Stilton-style blue cheeses. The combination of honey or nuts with the cheese and fruit also provides a delicious taste sensation.

The savoury, tangy, saltiness of Stilton is accompanied by a creamy, buttery flavour and texture that requires careful pairing with bread. Rye bread has a great combination of sweetness and rich maltiness that pairs well with Stilton-style blue cheeses, but it can be expensive and sometimes more difficult to obtain, so granary bread provides a similar pairing with a hint more nuttiness that works equally well.

Colston Bassett Stilton with Fig and Honey

This Stilton is made by Billy Kevan and the team at Colston Bassett Dairy, in the village of the same name in the Vale of Belvoir, Nottinghamshire. They have been making cheese since 1913 and their Stilton has won numerous awards for its quality and taste. Pasteurised milk is sourced from members of a farming co-operative, all of whom are situated within 1½ miles of the dairy. The cheese is made with either traditional or vegetarian rennet, depending on where it is sold.

Smooth and creamy, it has a rich, mellow flavour that is perfectly complemented by the sweetness and texture of the delicate figs, with honey adding a further layer of taste in this delicious recipe.

Ingredients

1 medium slice of rye or granary bread

75g Colston Bassett Stilton cheese, crumbled

1 large ripe fig, thinly sliced

2 teaspoons runny honey

Method

❖ Preheat the oven to 180°C/160°C fan/gas 4.

❖ Toast the bread on both sides and then place on a small baking tray.

❖ Spread the cheese over one side of the toast. Arrange the fig slices on top, then drizzle over the honey.

❖ Warm through in the oven for a few minutes, then transfer under the medium-hot grill until the cheese has melted and is starting to bubble and the fig slices are starting to caramelise.

●

Other cheeses that can be used in this recipe

Stilton-style blue cheeses
Cropwell Bishop, Stichelton, Hartington Shropshire Blue

Blue cheeses
Beauvale, Blue Murder, Young Buck, Renegade Monk, Cornish Blue, Barkham Blue, Norbury Blue, Cote Hill Blue

Cropwell Bishop Stilton with Port, Cranberries and Walnuts

This Stilton is made by cousins Robin and Ben Skailes and the team at Cropwell Bishop Creamery in the Vale of Belvoir, Nottinghamshire. Milk is supplied by 13 local farms and, as with all Stiltons, is pasteurised before being made into the cheese using vegetarian rennet. It has been made by the same method since the seventeenth century. After 12 weeks' maturing, the blue veins have developed and the cheese has a melt in the mouth, velvety, soft texture. The flavour is rich and tangy, with less sweetness than other Stiltons.

Combining the cheese with port-soaked cranberries and walnuts gives a delicious flavour when served on malty rye or granary toast.

Ingredients

50g dried cranberries

2 tablespoons ruby port

1 medium slice of rye or granary bread

75g Cropwell Bishop Stilton cheese, crumbled

50g walnut pieces

Method

❖ Place the cranberries in a small bowl, pour over the port and leave to soak for at least 2 hours.

❖ Preheat the oven to 180°C/160°C fan/gas 4.

❖ Toast the bread on both sides and then place on a small baking tray.

❖ Spread the cheese on one side of the toast. Drain the cranberries (see Tip) and scatter them over the cheese. Arrange the walnuts on top.

❖ Warm through in the oven for a few minutes, then transfer under the medium-hot grill until the cheese has melted and is starting to bubble (being careful not to let the nuts burn).

Tip – Drizzle any leftover port (from soaking the cranberries) over the cheese, too, if you like.

•

Other cheeses that can be used in this recipe

Stilton-style blue cheeses
Colston Bassett, Stichelton, Hartington Shropshire Blue

Blue cheeses
Beauvale, Blue Murder, Young Buck, Renegade Monk, Cornish Blue, Barkham Blue, Norbury Blue, Cote Hill Blue

Stichelton with Pear and Pecans

Stichelton is made by Joe Schneider and his team at Stichelton Dairy on Collingthwaite Farm on the Welbeck Estate, Nottinghamshire. The name Stichelton is an ancient name for the village of Stilton. Because this cheese is made using traditional rennet and unpasteurised milk from the farm itself, it cannot be called Stilton, as the PDO specifies pasteurised milk. Joe's belief that unpasteurised milk gives a superior cheese means that he had to use an alternative name. The cheese has a rich, buttery, soft, creamy texture with milky, savoury and sweet, nutty flavours.

Pairing with pears and pecans emphasises the flavours in the cheese in this tasty recipe.

Ingredients

1 medium slice of rye or granary bread

75g Stichelton cheese, crumbled

1 pear, peeled, cored and sliced

50g pecan nuts, finely chopped (see Tip)

Method

❖ Preheat the oven to 180°C/160°C fan/gas 4.

❖ Toast the bread on both sides and then place on a small baking tray.

❖ Spread the cheese on one side of the toast. Lay the pear slices over the cheese. Sprinkle the pecans on top.

❖ Warm through in the oven for a few minutes, then transfer under the medium-hot grill until the cheese has melted and is starting to bubble and the pear slices are lightly browned (being careful not to let the nuts burn).

Tip – Walnut pieces are a good alternative to pecans in this recipe.

•

Other cheeses that can be used in this recipe

Stilton-style blue cheeses
Colston Bassett, Cropwell Bishop, Hartington
Shropshire Blue

Blue cheeses
Beauvale, Blue Murder, Young Buck, Renegade Monk, Cornish Blue, Barkham Blue, Norbury Blue, Cote Hill Blue

Hartington Shropshire Blue with Pickled Walnuts and Chives

Made by Alan Salt and the team at Hartington Creamery on Pikehall Farm in Matlock, Derbyshire, they are the smallest and newest of the six registered Stilton makers and the only ones in Derbyshire. Never made in the county that gives it the name, Shropshire Blue was actually created in Scotland and is now made by several Stilton makers, including this version from Hartington. It is made using pasteurised milk from local herds and traditional rennet, in a similar manner to Stilton. Coloured with annatto natural vegetable colouring, the cheese is softer and creamier than Stilton and has a sharp, strong flavour.

Pickled walnuts and chives work together with the tanginess of the cheese to create this strong, full-flavoured recipe.

Ingredients

1 medium slice of rye or granary bread

75g Hartington Shropshire Blue cheese, crumbled

3 pickled walnuts, drained and sliced

1 teaspoon snipped fresh chives

Method

❖ Preheat the oven to 180°C/160°C fan/gas 4.

❖ Toast the bread on both sides and then place on a small baking tray.

❖ Spread the cheese on one side of the toast. Lay the pickled walnut slices over the cheese.

❖ Warm through in the oven for a few minutes, then transfer under the medium-hot grill until the cheese has melted and is starting to bubble and the pickled walnut slices are lightly browned (being careful not to let them burn).

❖ Sprinkle the snipped chives on top just before serving.

•

Other cheeses that can be used in this recipe

Stilton-style blue cheeses
Colston Bassett, Cropwell Bishop, Stichelton

Blue cheeses
Beauvale, Blue Murder, Young Buck, Renegade Monk, Cornish Blue, Barkham Blue, Norbury Blue, Cote Hill Blue

OTHER BLUE CHEESES

The previous chapter featured Stilton-style cheeses, but England also produces a wide and diverse range of other blue cheese styles. Ranging from the mild and creamy to the strong, salty and tangy, they all share one common feature, the mould that is used to make them. All of the moulds are in the *Penicillium* family, with the most common being *Penicillium roqueforti*, but *Penicillium glaucum* is sometimes used.

The origins of blue cheese can't be proven but legends suggest two possible sources. The first one suggests that a drunken cheesemaker left a half-eaten loaf of bread in a cave and when he returned the bread had developed a blue-coloured mould which transferred to the cheese. The second story relates specifically to Roquefort, one of the world's oldest blue cheeses, whereby a young shepherd boy was eating sheep's milk cheese in a cave, when his attention was distracted by a beautiful girl whom he chased after. When he returned, the cheese had turned blue. Whatever the true story, it is clear that the damp, humid conditions in certain caves allow spores of the *Penicillium* mould to thrive and prosper.

The *Penicillium* mould has now been cultured for use in cheesemaking and is added to the curd during manufacture. For the cheese to develop its blue veins, the mould requires oxygen. The cheese is therefore pierced with thin rods, which allow the oxygen to enter the holes that are left behind and start the development of the characteristic blue veining. As the mould grows, the grey-blue streaking appears along with the distinctive tangy blue flavour. This process usually takes between 3–6 months, with the veining starting at the centre of the cheese and working out towards the rind.

The blue cheeses in this section vary from mild, creamy and buttery to strong and tangy flavours. Each of the recipes has been designed to complement the variety of flavours, so a bread is needed that gives sufficient sweetness to contrast the blue tanginess whilst having a texture and flavour to stand up to the intensity. Wholemeal bread provides an ideal balance for this purpose.

The exception is the Young Buck with Chestnuts recipe, which has been prepared using soda bread, to complement the sweetness of the chestnuts and to maintain the strong Irish connection.

Beauvale with Dates

Beauvale was created as a new English cheese in 2011 by Robin Skailes and Howard Lucas of Cropwell Bishop Creamery in Nottinghamshire, to complement their world-class Stilton. It is made using pasteurised milk from 13 local farms with traditional rennet. It has a soft, melt in the mouth texture and mellow flavour similar to an Italian Gorgonzola and can simply be spread on the toast. It is perfect for lovers of more traditional English blue cheeses like Stilton but is also enjoyed by people who prefer a milder blue flavour.

For this recipe, most varieties of dates can be used, but the plump, soft, chewy Medjool variety is recommended as their caramel-like flavour complements the mild saltiness of the Beauvale perfectly.

Ingredients

1 medium slice of wholemeal bread

75g Beauvale cheese

4 Medjool dates, halved lengthways and stoned

Method

❖ Preheat the oven to 180°C/160°C fan/gas 4.

❖ Toast the bread on both sides and then place on a small baking tray.

❖ Spread the cheese on one side of the toast. Lay the date halves over the cheese.

❖ Warm through in the oven for a few minutes, then transfer under the medium-hot grill until the cheese has melted and is starting to bubble and the dates are starting to caramelise.

Other cheeses that can be used in this recipe

Stilton-style blue cheeses
Colston Bassett, Cropwell Bishop, Stichelton, Hartington Shropshire Blue

Blue cheeses
Blue Murder, Young Buck, Renegade Monk, Cornish Blue, Barkham Blue, Norbury Blue, Cote Hill Blue

Blue Murder with Apricots

Blue Murder is made by Rory Stone of Highland Fine Cheeses in Tain on the Dornoch Firth in the Scottish Highlands. Using pasteurised milk from local Holstein-Friesian cows and vegetarian rennet, this cheese is unusually shaped as a cube and wrapped in a saltire-design foil. It is softer and creamier than many blues, with a texture more closely related to Italian Gorgonzola than a traditional British blue cheese, which enables it simply to be spread on the toast. The cheese has a thin and sticky, grey-white rind with a pale ivory centre containing purple-blue veins, and a mild tangy flavour with a hint of sweetness.

Pairing it with the sweet sharpness of apricots gives a great taste combination in this recipe.

Ingredients

1 medium slice of wholemeal bread

75g Blue Murder cheese

3 fresh ripe apricots, halved and stoned (see Tip)

Method

❖ Preheat the oven to 180°C/160°C fan/gas 4.

❖ Toast the bread on both sides and then place on a small baking tray.

❖ Spread the cheese on one side of the toast. Lay the apricot halves over the cheese, cut-sides down.

❖ Warm through in the oven for a few minutes, then transfer under the medium-hot grill until the cheese has melted and is starting to bubble and the apricots are starting to caramelise.

Tip – If you can't find fresh apricots, swap them for 1–2 small ripe peaches or nectarines.

Other cheeses that can be used in this recipe

Stilton-style blue cheeses
Colston Bassett, Cropwell Bishop, Stichelton, Hartington Shropshire Blue

Blue cheeses
Beauvale, Young Buck, Renegade Monk, Cornish Blue, Barkham Blue, Norbury Blue, Cote Hill Blue

Young Buck with Chestnuts

Made by Michael Thomson of Mike's Fancy Cheese Company in Newtownards, County Down, Northern Ireland, Young Buck is a relatively new cheese made to a Stilton-style recipe. It is the first unpasteurised milk cheese made in Northern Ireland using milk from a local herd and traditional rennet. After hand-ladling into moulds, the cheeses are pierced to allow the blue veins to develop and form rich, creamy but tangy cheeses.

The natural sweetness and nuttiness of the chestnuts and the buttermilk in the soda bread pair well with the salty tanginess of the cheese in this tasty recipe.

Ingredients

1 medium slice of soda bread

75g Young Buck cheese, crumbled

4 peeled and roasted whole chestnuts, roughly chopped (see Tip)

Method

- ❖ Preheat the oven to 180°C/160°C fan/gas 4.

- ❖ Toast the bread on both sides and then place on a small baking tray.

- ❖ Spread the cheese on one side of the toast. Scatter the chestnuts over the top.

- ❖ Warm through in the oven for a few minutes, then transfer under the medium-hot grill until the cheese has melted and is starting to bubble (being careful not to let the chestnuts burn).

Tip – Swap the roasted chestnuts for 16 walnut halves (about 30g).

•

Other cheeses that can be used in this recipe

Stilton-style blue cheeses
Colston Bassett, Cropwell Bishop, Stichelton, Hartington Shropshire Blue

Blue cheeses
Beauvale, Blue Murder, Renegade Monk, Cornish Blue, Barkham Blue, Norbury Blue, Cote Hill Blue

Renegade Monk with Fruitcake

Made by Penelope Nagle and Marcus Fergusson at Feltham's Farm in Templecombe, Somerset, this is a modern cheese, having only been launched in 2017. Using pasteurised organic milk from a local herd, it is made using vegetarian rennet. After making the small cheeses, they are washed in Hop Drop organic ale from Stroud Brewery to enhance the flavour even further during the four-week maturation. The cheese has a light blue veining with a strong, fruity flavour from the ale-washed rind.

Pairing this tangy, pungent cheese with the sweet richness of fruitcake creates an interesting and powerful combination of flavours.

Ingredients

1 medium slice of wholemeal bread

50g slice of rich fruitcake, crumbled

75g Renegade Monk cheese, thinly sliced

Method

❖ Preheat the oven to 180°C/160°C fan/gas 4.

❖ Toast the bread on both sides and then place on a small baking tray.

❖ Crumble the fruitcake over one side of the toast. Lay the cheese slices on top.

❖ Warm through in the oven for a few minutes, then transfer under the medium-hot grill until the cheese has melted and is starting to bubble.

●

Other cheeses that can be used in this recipe

Stilton-style blue cheeses
Colston Bassett, Cropwell Bishop, Stichelton, Hartington Shropshire Blue

Blue cheeses
Beauvale, Blue Murder, Young Buck, Cornish Blue, Barkham Blue, Norbury Blue, Cote Hill Blue

Cornish Blue with Tenderstem Broccoli and Almonds

Made by Phil Stansfield and the team at Cornish Blue Cheese Company at Knowle Farm near Liskeard on the edge of Bodmin Moor in Cornwall. Using unpasteurised milk from their own herd of Holstein-Friesians and vegetarian rennet, this cheese has previously won the World Champion Cheese Award. Maturing for 12 weeks results in a cheese with a rich, buttery texture and a mild, creamy nuttiness and slight sweetness, which is not as salty or tangy as many other blue cheeses.

Pairing the cheese with the almonds in this recipe matches the nuttiness, and the slightly sweet freshness of the charred broccoli adds a further taste and texture contrast.

Ingredients

50g blanched flaked almonds

1 teaspoon olive oil

4 tenderstem broccoli stems, trimmed

1 medium slice of wholemeal bread

75g Cornish Blue cheese, sliced

Method

❖ Toast the almonds in a small, dry frying pan over a low heat for a few minutes or until lightly browned, shaking the pan to keep them moving (don't leave them unattended as they will burn easily). Tip onto a plate and set aside.

❖ Heat the olive oil in the same frying pan (or a griddle pan), add the broccoli and cook over a medium heat, turning regularly, until lightly charred, about 5 minutes.

❖ Meanwhile, preheat the grill to medium-high. Toast the bread on both sides and then place on a small baking tray.

❖ Arrange the broccoli and almonds over one side of the toast. Lay the cheese slices on top.

❖ Place under the preheated grill until the cheese has melted and is starting to bubble.

•

Other cheeses that can be used in this recipe

Stilton-style blue cheeses
Colston Bassett, Cropwell Bishop, Stichelton, Hartington Shropshire Blue

Blue cheeses
Beauvale, Blue Murder, Young Buck, Renegade Monk, Barkham Blue, Norbury Blue, Cote Hill Blue

Barkham Blue with Greek Honey

Made by Andy, Sandy and Nia Rose at Two Hoots Cheese in Barkham, Berkshire, using pasteurised milk from a local herd of Jersey and Guernsey cows and vegetarian rennet. The creamy Channel Island milk gives a buttery richness to the unusual ammonite-shaped cheese, which is covered in a dark, rustic rind. The cheese itself is golden yellow and has a rich, buttery, melt in the mouth texture, which enables it simply to be spread on the toast.

Combining the buttery richness with the aromatic qualities of Greek honey makes for a truly delicious flavour that is enhanced by the sweet nuttiness of the wholemeal bread. This is a simple but extremely tasty recipe.

Ingredients

1 medium slice of wholemeal bread

75g Barkham Blue cheese

2 tablespoons Greek honey (see Tip)

Method

❖ Preheat the grill to medium-high.

❖ Toast the bread on both sides and then place on a small baking tray.

❖ Spread the cheese on one side of the toast. Drizzle the honey over the cheese.

❖ Place under the preheated grill until the cheese has melted and is starting to bubble.

Tip – Greek honey is the top choice here, but why not try using your favourite honey instead?

Other cheeses that can be used in this recipe

Stilton-style blue cheeses
Colston Bassett, Cropwell Bishop, Stichelton, Hartington Shropshire Blue

Blue cheeses
Beauvale, Blue Murder, Young Buck, Renegade Monk, Cornish Blue, Norbury Blue, Cote Hill Blue

Norbury Blue with Jam Packed Real Ale Chutney

Norbury Blue is the creation of Michaela and Neil Allam at Norbury Park Farm Cheeses in Surrey. Unpasteurised milk from a local herd of Holstein-Friesian cows is used with vegetarian rennet. It is a tangy blue cheese with a rich, creamy texture that melts in the mouth. Michaela and Neil are real ale lovers and with Tillingbourne Brewery being located on the same Albury Estate, it seemed natural for them to have their real ale chutney made with their favourite local ale. It is sold as 'Jam Packed Real Ale Chutney' and is used in this recipe.

Watercress is also used, as Neil is a former watercress grower from Hampshire, and the peppery leaves provide a tasty contrast to the creamy cheese and fruity chutney.

Ingredients

1 medium slice of wholemeal bread

25g Jam Packed Real Ale Chutney (see Tip)

a small handful of watercress

75g Norbury Blue cheese

Method

❖ Preheat the oven to 180°C/160°C fan/gas 4.

❖ Toast the bread on both sides and then place on a small baking tray.

❖ Spread the chutney on one side of the toast, then lay the watercress on top. Crumble the cheese over the watercress.

❖ Warm through in the oven for a few minutes, then transfer under the medium-hot grill until the cheese has melted and is starting to bubble.

Tip – Jam Packed Real Ale Chutney has been chosen for this recipe as the makers are located on the same estate as the cheesemaker, but if you have a favourite fruit chutney, why not try that instead?

●

Other cheeses that can be used in this recipe

Stilton-style blue cheeses
Colston Bassett, Cropwell Bishop, Stichelton, Hartington Shropshire Blue

Blue cheeses
Beauvale, Blue Murder, Young Buck, Renegade Monk, Cornish Blue, Barkham Blue, Cote Hill Blue

Cote Hill Blue with Toasted Walnuts
and Mandarin

This blue cheese is made by Mary and Michael Davenport of Cote Hill Cheese at Cote Hill Farm in Osgodby, Lincolnshire, using unpasteurised milk from their own herd of Holstein-Friesian and Brown Swiss cows and vegetarian rennet. One of the few unpasteurised soft blue cheeses made in Britain, it is matured for two months allowing a firm rind to develop. The centre is much softer than most blues with a texture often likened to a Brie and a flavour that is milder and creamier than most but still retaining the blue tanginess.

The sweet, toasted nuttiness of walnuts and the fruity tanginess of mandarin make for a delicious combination.

Ingredients

20g unsalted butter

50g walnut pieces

1 medium slice of wholemeal bread

½ × 300g can (90g drained weight) mandarin segments in juice (see Tips)

75g Cote Hill Blue cheese

Method

❖ Preheat the oven to 180°C/160°C fan/gas 4.

❖ Melt the butter in a small saucepan, add the walnuts and cook over a low heat for about 5 minutes or until lightly toasted, stirring regularly.

❖ Toast the bread on both sides and then place on a small baking tray.

❖ Spoon the toasted walnuts and any buttery juices over one side of the toast. Place the mandarin segments in amongst the walnuts. Crumble the cheese over the top.

❖ Warm through in the oven for a few minutes, then transfer under the medium-hot grill until the cheese has melted and is starting to bubble.

Tips – To use the leftover mandarin segments, grill them under a low heat until caramelised, then leave to cool and serve them as an accompaniment to your cheeseboard, or simply use the segments (straight from the can) in a fruit salad.

•

Other cheeses that can be used in this recipe

Stilton-style blue cheeses
Colston Bassett, Cropwell Bishop, Stichelton, Hartington Shropshire Blue

Blue cheeses
Beauvale, Blue Murder, Young Buck, Renegade Monk, Cornish Blue, Barkham Blue, Norbury Blue

GOAT'S MILK CHEESES

Goat's milk cheeses are made in the same way as their cow's milk counterparts by coagulating the solids in the milk, separating the solids or curds from the liquid whey and then forming them into the desired shape before maturing. In the case of goat's milk, it can be coagulated with either rennet, as with most other cheeses, or with an acid such as vinegar or lemon juice, which results in a very soft-textured cheese.

Goat's milk cheeses will always be pure white compared to the typically yellow colour of cow's milk cheeses and cream colour of sheep's milk cheeses. This colour difference is due to a pigment called beta-carotene that occurs naturally in many fruits and vegetables, but also in grass. Cows are not able to metabolise the beta-carotene, hence the yellow colour in the cheese, but goats convert all of it to vitamin A, which is colourless, hence the pure white colour of the cheese.

Goat's milk has a similar level of fats to cow's milk but has a higher concentration of fatty acids, which causes the distinctive tangy, tart flavour. Containing less milk protein than cow's milk, goat's milk produces a smoother, creamier texture, and means that goat's cheese is physically different to cow's cheese, mainly due to its lack of strength internally. It would be almost impossible to make a stretchy cheese like mozzarella or to make a brittle, hard cheese from goat's milk. Even the hardest of goat's milk cheeses are still either semi-hard or firm and never fully hard. Likewise, goat's milk cheeses mature much faster than their cow's milk counterparts.

Goat's milk cheeses have numerous nutritional benefits, but the most significant one is that they have a different protein structure to cow's milk cheeses and are naturally lower in lactose. This means that they can be more easily digested by people who have any form of lactose intolerance.

Due to the savoury, tangy and tart flavours common to all goat's cheeses, a bread with a similar flavour profile will work best with them. Sourdough meets this requirement exactly and provides an excellent pairing.

Golden Cross with Tapenade

Made by Kevin and Alison Blunt of Golden Cross Cheese Company at Greenacres Farm in Holmes Hill, East Sussex, using unpasteurised milk from their own herd of British Saanen, Toggenburg and British Alpine goats and vegetarian rennet. The small log-shaped cheese is based on similar styles from the Loire valley, which is rolled in ash and ripened for three weeks to allow the soft, wrinkled, white rind to develop. The interior is silky smooth and delicate with a fresh citrus flavour.

The unusual pairing with salty, tangy tapenade makes for a full flavour combination in this recipe.

Ingredients

1 medium slice of sourdough bread

1 garlic clove, halved

2 tablespoons black olive tapenade (see Tip)

75g Golden Cross cheese, cut into thin discs

Method

❖ Preheat the grill to medium-high.

❖ Toast the bread on both sides and then place on a small baking tray.

❖ Rub the garlic halves over one side of the hot toast. Spread the tapenade over the same side of the toast.

❖ Lay the cheese discs over the tapenade, covering it completely.

❖ Place under the preheated grill until the cheese has melted and turned golden brown.

Tip – Green pesto is a tasty alternative to the tapenade in this recipe.

•

Other cheeses that can be used in this recipe

Soft goat's milk cheeses
Ragstone, Rosary, Cerney Ash, Ticklemore, Sinodun Hill, White Nancy

Soft sheep's milk cheeses
Wigmore, Riseley, Flower Marie, Sussex Slipcote

Ragstone with Toasted Almonds

One of a range of soft goat's milk cheeses made at Neal's Yard Creamery in Herefordshire, this cheese uses pasteurised goat's milk from a nearby herd and traditional rennet. The small log shape is based on cheeses from the Loire valley, and is coated in a soft, wrinkled, white rind, which develops during the three-week maturing. It has a smooth, creamy texture and a faintly citrus, nutty flavour with a lingering finish.

Pairing the cheese with the sweet nuttiness of toasted almonds gives not only a great flavour combination but also a contrast in textures.

Ingredients

1 medium slice of sourdough bread

75g Ragstone cheese, cut into thin discs

50g blanched flaked almonds

2 teaspoons runny honey

Method

❖ Preheat the grill to medium-high.

❖ Toast the bread on both sides and then place on a small baking tray.

❖ Lay the cheese discs on one side of the toast, then sprinkle the flaked almonds over the top.

❖ Place under the preheated grill until the cheese has melted and turned golden brown and the almonds are lightly toasted (being careful not to let them burn).

❖ Drizzle over the honey just before serving.

•

Other cheeses that can be used in this recipe

Soft goat's milk cheeses
Golden Cross, Rosary, Cerney Ash, Ticklemore, Sinodun Hill, White Nancy

Soft sheep's milk cheeses
Wigmore, Riseley, Flower Marie, Sussex Slipcote

Rosary with Greyfriars Rosé Reserve-soaked Raspberries

Made by Chris and Claire Moody at Rosary Goats Cheese in Landford, Wiltshire, using pasteurised milk from local herds of Saanen goats and vegetarian rennet, to create this delicious log-shaped cheese. It has a silky-soft, creamy texture with no rind and a fresh lemony flavour.

The tangy creaminess of the cheese is paired with the sweet, slightly sharp, boozy, wine-soaked raspberries in this recipe. Greyfriars Rosé Reserve is a delicious English sparkling wine made by Mike Wagstaff and the team at Greyfriars Vineyard in the Surrey Hills. After soaking the raspberries, the leftover wine can be enjoyed as a perfect accompaniment to this tasty recipe.

Ingredients

75g fresh raspberries

100ml Greyfriars Rosé Reserve sparkling wine

1 medium slice of sourdough bread

75g Rosary cheese, thinly sliced

Method

❖ Put the raspberries into a small bowl, pour over the wine and leave to soak for 2 hours.

❖ Preheat the grill to medium-high.

❖ Toast the bread on both sides and then place on a small baking tray.

❖ Drain the raspberries (see intro), then spread them out over one side of the toast, squashing them slightly as you go. Lay the cheese discs on top.

❖ Place under the preheated grill until the cheese has melted and turned golden brown.

Other cheeses that can be used in this recipe

Soft goat's milk cheeses
Golden Cross, Ragstone, Cerney Ash, Ticklemore, Sinodun Hill, White Nancy

Soft sheep's milk cheeses
Wigmore, Riseley, Flower Marie, Sussex Slipcote

Cerney Ash with Hampshire Salami and Balsamic Figs

This cheese is made by Avril Pratt in the village of Cerney, in Gloucestershire, using unpasteurised milk from local Cotswold goat herds and vegetarian rennet. It was originally made by Lady Isabel Angus in the butler's pantry at Cerney House, but growth meant the business moved to nearby Chapel Farm and the company is still run by her family today. The cheeses are based on Valencay from the Loire Valley, with the traditional flat-topped pyramid shape. Each cheese has a soft rind coated in a mixture of oak ash and sea salt.

The salami is a British version of a traditional Italian sausage made from hand-cured local pork by The Hampshire Salami Company. This recipe uses their Sopressa Salami due to its soft texture. The umami, sweet balsamic figs work with the citrus freshness of the cheese and the spicy salami to give a wonderful combination of flavours.

Ingredients

2 fresh figs, cut in half lengthways

2 teaspoons demerara sugar

2 tablespoons balsamic vinegar

1 medium slice of sourdough bread

4 thin slices Hampshire Sopressa Salami (see Tip)

75g Cerney Ash cheese, sliced

Method

❖ Lay the fig halves, cut-sides up, in a dry frying pan, then sprinkle over the sugar. Cook over a high heat for about 3 minutes until the sugar has melted, then flip the figs over and remove the pan from the heat. Drizzle the balsamic vinegar over the figs and swirl the pan to make a syrup.

❖ Meanwhile, preheat the grill to medium-high. Toast the bread on both sides and then place on a small baking tray.

❖ Lay the salami slices over one side of the toast. Top with the fig halves and syrup. Lay the cheese slices on top.

❖ Place under the preheated grill until the cheese has melted and turned golden brown.

Tip – Milanese Salami or Finnochiona Salami (fennel-flavoured) instead of the Sopressa Salami work well in this recipe, too.

•

Other cheeses that can be used in this recipe

Soft goat's milk cheeses
Golden Cross, Ragstone, Rosary, Ticklemore, Sinodun Hill, White Nancy

Soft sheep's milk cheeses
Wigmore, Riseley, Flower Marie, Sussex Slipcote

Rachel with Anchovies

White Lake Cheese is famed for its range of goat's milk cheeses made using unpasteurised milk from their own herd of Toggenburg, British Alpine and Saanen goats and vegetarian rennet, but Roger Longman is probably best known for his iconic Rachel cheese. He created this semi-hard, washed-rind cheese, named after a friend who he described as being similar to the cheese in that it is sweet, curvy and nutty. The texture is firm but creamy with a savoury, sweet flavour that is fresh, milky, buttery and nutty.

In this recipe, the unusual but very simple pairing with anchovies gives an amazing taste sensation.

Ingredients

1 medium slice of sourdough bread

75g Rachel cheese, thinly sliced

½ × 50g can (15g drained weight) anchovies in olive oil (see Tips)

Method

* Preheat the grill to medium-high.

* Toast the bread on both sides and then place on a small baking tray.

* Lay the cheese slices over one side of the toast. Arrange the anchovies on top of the cheese in a criss-cross pattern.

* Place under the preheated grill until the cheese has melted and the anchovies have started to melt.

Tips – To use the leftover half can of anchovies, why not make another slice of cheese on toast for a friend (or for yourself, if hungry)? Anchovies are also fantastic for adding flavour to a pizza. Store the leftover anchovies in a sealed container (covered with the original oil from the can) in the fridge for up to 2 days.

Other cheeses that can be used in this recipe

Firm sheep's milk cheeses
Berkswell, Lord of the Hundreds, Corra Linn

Ticklemore with Fresh Dill

First created by the legendary cheesemaker, Robin Congdon, the recipe was passed onto Sharpham Creamery in Totnes, Devon, where Greg and Nicky Parsons and the team now make this delicious goat's cheese. Using pasteurised milk from a herd of Saanen, Toggenburg and Anglo-Nubian goats at Button Farm on Dartmoor, the cheese is traditionally made using vegetarian rennet. Two months' maturing results in a cheese with a soft, white rind and a pure white, chalky interior. The flavour is rich and clean with a fresh, lemony tang and salty finish.

The aromatic freshness of dill makes for an excellent partner to the cheese in this tasty recipe.

Ingredients

1 medium slice of sourdough bread

6 fresh dill sprigs (see Tip)

2 teaspoons tomato purée (use the sun-dried version for a more intense flavour)

75g Ticklemore cheese, sliced

2 teaspoons pine nuts

Method

❖ Preheat the grill to medium-high.

❖ Toast the bread on both sides and then place on a small baking tray.

❖ Strip the fronds of dill from the stalks and discard the stalks. Spread the tomato purée on one side of the toast. Sprinkle the dill fronds over.

❖ Lay the cheese slices on top, then sprinkle the pine nuts over.

❖ Place under the preheated grill until the cheese has melted and turned golden brown and the pine nuts are lightly browned (being careful not to let them burn).

Tip – Dill can be swapped for fresh parsley or thyme, if you prefer.

•

Other cheeses that can be used in this recipe

Soft goat's milk cheeses
Golden Cross, Ragstone, Rosary, Cerney Ash, Sinodun Hill, White Nancy

Soft sheep's milk cheeses
Wigmore, Riseley, Flower Marie, Sussex Slipcote

Sinodun Hill with Marmalade

Made by Fraser Norton and Rachel Yarrow at Earth Trust Farm near Shillingford, Oxfordshire, using unpasteurised milk from their own herd of Anglo-Nubian goats and vegetarian rennet. The cheese is made as a flattened pyramid shape before being matured for two weeks until the rind forms with a soft, white, wrinkly appearance, sometimes mottled with blue and grey edible moulds. The texture is delicate, smooth, rich and creamy with flavours of citrus and herbs.

The bitter sweetness of marmalade combined with the warm spiciness of the cinnamon gives an amazing taste combination here.

Ingredients

1 medium slice of sourdough bread

about 30g marmalade of choice (or enough to cover the toast)

75g Sinodun Hill cheese

1 teaspoon ground cinnamon

Method

- ❖ Preheat the grill to medium-high.

- ❖ Toast the bread on both sides and then place on a small baking tray.

- ❖ Spread the marmalade on one side of the toast. Spread the cheese on top, then sprinkle the cinnamon over.

- ❖ Place under the preheated grill until the cheese has melted and turned golden brown.

Other cheeses that can be used in this recipe

Soft goat's milk cheeses
Golden Cross, Ragstone, Rosary, Cerney Ash, Ticklemore, White Nancy

Soft sheep's milk cheeses
Wigmore, Riseley, Flower Marie, Sussex Slipcote

White Nancy with Roasted Red Peppers

Roger Longman at White Lake Cheese in Somerset uses unpasteurised milk from his own herd of Toggenburg, British Alpine and Saanen goats and vegetarian rennet. He has created this mild and crumbly cheese, named after a local landmark in the Cheshire village where his former cheesemaker grew up. The White Nancy landmark was named after the daughter of the landmark's builder and was erected to celebrate the Battle of Waterloo. The texture is semi-soft and has a slightly sweet citrusy flavour.

The sweetness of the roasted red peppers and salty capers provide a great combination in this recipe.

Ingredients

1 medium slice of sourdough bread

50g (drained weight) roasted red peppers in oil (from a jar), cut into 1cm strips

2 teaspoons capers, drained and chopped

75g White Nancy cheese, sliced

Method

❖ Preheat the oven to 180°C/160°C fan/gas 4.

❖ Toast the bread on both sides and then place on a small baking tray.

❖ Lay the peppers over one side of the toast, then drizzle over a little oil from the jar. Scatter the capers over the peppers. Lay the cheese slices on top.

❖ Warm through in the oven for a few minutes, then transfer under the medium-hot grill until the cheese has melted and turned golden brown.

●

Other cheeses that can be used in this recipe

Soft goat's milk cheeses
Golden Cross, Ragstone, Rosary, Cerney Ash, Ticklemore, Sinodun Hill

Soft sheep's milk cheeses
Wigmore, Riseley, Flower Marie, Sussex Slipcote

SHEEP'S MILK CHEESES

Sheep's or ewe's milk is especially suited to making cheese despite the significantly lower yields from sheep, who only have two teats and produce approximately one-tenth as much milk as a cow. The milk from a sheep has numerous other benefits for the cheesemaker. It contains twice as much butterfat and 70 per cent more protein, resulting in a much higher yield of solids and therefore more cheese produced for the same quantity of milk. The higher solid yield means that only 50–70 per cent as much milk is needed to make the same quantity of cheese, compared to using cow's milk.

Sheep's milk is also more digestible due to the fat and protein molecules being smaller, plus it has twice the goodness of cow's milk and 3–4 times as much calcium. It does, however, contain similar levels of lactose, but the presence of more short-chain fatty acids leads to higher lactose absorption and therefore easier digestion. This is because all of the lactose is converted to acid by the lactic acid bacteria used in the cheesemaking process.

The higher levels of fat and protein result in a cheese that is rich and usually tangy. Flavours are usually slightly sweet and often reminiscent of caramel or butterscotch.

Sheep's milk is used throughout the world to make a whole range of cheese styles, including soft, creamy cheeses, washed-rind cheeses, firm Cheddar-style cheeses, hard, brittle crumbly-styles and even blue cheeses.

Some of the world's most iconic cheeses are made from sheep's milk, amongst them being Feta, Manchego and Roquefort, and Britain is now producing cheeses in all these styles, some of which feature in the following recipes.

Richer than cow's milk cheeses and with their distinctive tanginess, sheep's milk cheeses pair perfectly with the savoury tanginess of sourdough.

Wigmore with Roasted Grapes

Wigmore is named after its creator, Anne Wigmore, and is made by Village Maid Cheese in Berkshire (famous for its Waterloo cheese) using thermised milk from nearby herds of Dorset Friesland sheep and vegetarian rennet. The cheese is made by curd washing, a technique that gives the cheese its characteristic delicate, soft, oozing centre. The soft, white rind encloses a ripe, slightly sweet, smooth centre with a complex fruity richness of flavour.

Sweet, intense roasted grapes and aromatic thyme leaves provide an excellent match for the subtle creaminess of the cheese in this delicious recipe.

Ingredients

12 seedless black grapes, halved (see Tip)

1 teaspoon olive oil

2 teaspoons runny honey

1 medium slice of sourdough bread

1 teaspoon fresh thyme leaves

75g Wigmore cheese, thinly sliced

Method

❖ Preheat the oven to 180°C/160°C fan/gas 4.

❖ Place the grapes in an ovenproof dish, then drizzle over the olive oil and the honey. Roast in the oven for about 20 minutes or until the grapes start to burst, stirring a few times during cooking.

❖ Meanwhile, preheat the grill to medium-high. Toast the bread on both sides and then place on a small baking tray.

❖ Spoon the roasted grapes and their juices over one side of the toast, then sprinkle over the thyme leaves. Lay the cheese slices on top.

❖ Place under the preheated grill until the cheese has melted and is starting to bubble.

Tip – Try roasting cherries instead of grapes for this recipe (see Waterloo with Roasted Cherries recipe on page 49).

•

Other cheeses that can be used in this recipe

Soft sheep's milk cheeses
Riseley, Flower Marie, Sussex Slipcote

Soft goat's milk cheeses
Golden Cross, Ragstone, Rosary, Cerney Ash, Ticklemore, Sinodun Hill, White Nancy

Riseley with Parma Ham and Asparagus

Another sheep's milk cheese from the Wigmores at Village Maid Cheese in Berkshire. Made using thermised milk from local herds of Dorset Friesland sheep and vegetarian rennet, the cheese is named after the village where the dairy is located. Although the cheese itself is made at Village Maid, the ripening is carried out by Neal's Yard Dairy in their maturing rooms in Bermondsey, London, where they spend four weeks washing the young cheeses in brine every few days. This process develops a soft, sticky, pinky-orange rind, with a hint of salty crunch and a strong, savoury centre with a salty, slightly smoky flavour and a hint of fruitiness.

Pairing it with asparagus and salty ham provides a delicious contrast to the cheese in this recipe.

Ingredients

3 slices Parma ham

6 thin asparagus spears, trimmed

2 teaspoons olive oil

1 medium slice of sourdough bread

½ teaspoon freshly ground black pepper

75g Riseley cheese, thinly sliced

Method

❖ Wrap each slice of Parma ham around two asparagus spears.

❖ Heat the olive oil in a small frying pan over a medium heat until hot, then add the wrapped asparagus. Cook for about 5 minutes, turning a few times so that the Parma ham lightly browns all over.

❖ Meanwhile, preheat the grill to medium-high. Toast the bread on both sides and then place on a small baking tray.

❖ Arrange the ham-wrapped asparagus on one side of the toast, then sprinkle with the black pepper. Lay the cheese slices on top.

❖ Place under the preheated grill until the cheese has melted and is starting to bubble.

•

Other cheeses that can be used in this recipe

Soft sheep's milk cheeses
Wigmore, Flower Marie, Sussex Slipcote, St James

Washed-rind cheeses
Stinking Bishop, Rollright, Maida Vale, Golden Cenarth

Flower Marie with Dates and Nuts

Best known for their Golden Cross goat's cheese log, Kevin and Alison Blunt of Golden Cross Cheese Company in East Sussex have used unpasteurised milk from a herd of Friesland Dorset sheep, owned by Wayfield Dairy Sheep in Stratford-upon-Avon, and vegetarian rennet to create this deliciously soft cheese. Based on a recipe from legendary cheesemaker, James Aldridge, the cheese is made in a square shape with a soft, white rind. The texture is soft, rich and creamy, which softens further during ripening. Flavours are intense and complex with tastes of mushroom, citrus and fresh grass.

In this recipe, dates and toasted nuts provide a rich and full-flavoured contrast to the rich, creamy cheese.

Ingredients

1 tablespoon blanched whole almonds (see Tip)

1 tablespoon blanched whole hazelnuts

1 tablespoon walnut pieces

4 Medjool dates, stoned and roughly chopped

1 medium slice of sourdough bread

75g Flower Marie cheese, sliced

Method

❖ Put all the nuts into a small, dry frying pan. Toast over a low heat for a few minutes or until lightly browned, shaking the pan to keep them moving (don't leave them unattended as they will burn easily). Set aside to cool, then roughly chop and mix with the dates.

❖ Preheat the grill to medium-high. Toast the bread on both sides and then place on a small baking tray.

❖ Spoon the nut/date mix onto one side of the toast. Lay the cheese slices on top.

❖ Place under the preheated grill until the cheese has melted and is starting to bubble.

Tip – Any combination of unsalted nuts can be used, according to personal taste.

•

Other cheeses that can be used in this recipe

Soft sheep's milk cheeses
Wigmore, Riseley, Sussex Slipcote

Soft goat's milk cheeses
Golden Cross, Ragstone, Rosary, Cerney Ash,
Ticklemore, Sinodun Hill, White Nancy

Sussex Slipcote with Sunblush Tomatoes, Olives and Capers

Made by Mark and Sarah Hardy at High Weald Dairy on Tremains Farm in Horsted Keynes, West Sussex, using pasteurised organic milk from local herds of sheep and vegetarian rennet. The cheese is a fresh soft cheese made as either small buttons or large logs. It has a light, creamy and almost fluffy texture which is easily spreadable. The aroma and flavour is delicate and lemony with a mouthwatering acidity and freshness.

Pairing the cheese with sweet, umami-tasting sunblush tomatoes and salty, tangy olives and capers gives a delicious flavour to this recipe.

Ingredients

50g sunblush tomatoes, roughly chopped

30g (drained weight) pitted green olives, roughly chopped

2 teaspoons capers, drained

1 medium slice of sourdough bread

75g Sussex Slipcote cheese, sliced

Method

- ❖ Preheat the oven to 180°C/160°C fan/gas 4.

- ❖ Mix together the sunblush tomatoes, olives and capers.

- ❖ Toast the bread on both sides and then place on a small baking tray.

- ❖ Spoon the tomato mix onto one side of the toast. Lay the cheese slices on top.

- ❖ Warm through in the oven for a few minutes, then transfer under the medium-hot grill until the cheese has melted and is starting to bubble.

•

Other cheeses that can be used in this recipe

Soft sheep's milk cheeses
Wigmore, Riseley, Flower Marie

Soft goat's milk cheeses
Golden Cross, Ragstone, Rosary, Cerney Ash, Ticklemore, Sinodun Hill, White Nancy

Berkswell with Serrano Ham and Dates

Made by the Fletcher family and Julie Hay at Ram Hall Farm near Berkswell, West Midlands, using unpasteurised milk from their own herd of Friesland and Lacaune sheep and traditional rennet. After four months' maturing, the distinctive 'flying saucer'-shaped cheese develops a rustic, orange-brown rind and a firm, slightly crumbly texture with a hint of graininess similar to a Spanish Manchego. The flavours are savoury and fruity with nutty and caramel notes.

Pairing with the saltiness of the Spanish ham and the sweet, richness of the dates provides a tasty combination here.

Ingredients

4 slices Serrano ham (see Tip)

4 Medjool dates, cut in half lengthways and stoned

1 medium slice of sourdough bread

2 teaspoons olive oil

75g Berkswell cheese, sliced

Method

❖ Preheat the oven to 180°C/160°C fan/gas 4.

❖ Wrap each slice of ham around two date halves. Set aside.

❖ Toast the bread on both sides and then place on a small baking tray.

❖ Place the wrapped dates on one side of the toast, then drizzle over the olive oil. Lay the cheese slices on top.

❖ Warm through in the oven for a few minutes, then transfer under the medium-hot grill until the cheese has melted and is starting to bubble.

Tip – Swap in prosciutto or Parma ham for the Serrano ham, if you prefer.

•

Other cheeses that can be used in this recipe

Firm sheep's milk cheeses
Lord of the Hundreds, Corra Linn

Firm goat's milk cheeses
Rachel

St James with Quince Jelly

Martin Gott and Nicola Robinson at Holker Farm Dairy in Cartmel, Cumbria, make this unique British cheese, a washed-rind sheep's milk cheese. Martin learned cheesemaking by working with many of the best known British cheesemakers, and has named his iconic cheese after James Aldridge, the pioneer of rind-washing in Britain. It is made using unpasteurised milk from their own herd of Lacaune sheep and traditional rennet. The texture varies through the seasons, ranging from buttery soft to firm and chalky. Flavours are complex, rich, deep and have a malty sweetness.

The creamy texture and malty sweetness of the cheese pairs well with the sweet and sour flavour of the quince jelly in this recipe.

Ingredients

1 medium slice of sourdough bread

30g quince jelly

75g St James cheese, sliced

Method

❖ Preheat the grill to medium-high.

❖ Toast the bread on both sides and then place on a small baking tray.

❖ Spread the quince jelly over one side of the toast. Lay the cheese slices on top.

❖ Place under the preheated grill until the cheese has melted and is starting to bubble.

●

Other cheeses that can be used in this recipe

Soft sheep's milk cheeses
Wigmore, Riseley, Flower Marie, Sussex Slipcote

Washed-rind cheeses
Stinking Bishop, Rollright, Maida Vale, Golden Cenarth

Lord of the Hundreds British Carbonara on Toast

Made by the Delves family of The Traditional Cheese Dairy at Burnt House Farm in Horam, East Sussex, this cheese is named after an ancient tax collector. They use unpasteurised milk from sustainable family farms in the home counties, along with vegetarian rennet. It is a hard, natural-rinded, complex cheese that is shaped as a square and is matured for about nine months to give a hard, grainy texture similar to Italian sheep's cheeses.

The inspiration behind this recipe is Italian pasta carbonara, using smoked bacon instead of pancetta, with the toast replacing the pasta.

Ingredients

1 teaspoon olive oil

2 rashers smoked streaky bacon, diced (see Tip)

¼ onion, finely diced

1 garlic clove, crushed

2 tablespoons crème fraîche

50g Lord of the Hundreds cheese, grated

1 medium slice of sourdough bread

Method

❖ Heat the olive oil in a small frying pan, add the bacon and sauté gently until lightly browned but not crisp. Transfer to a plate and set aside.

❖ Add the onion and garlic to the same pan and cook over a medium heat until soft and transparent, about 5 minutes.

❖ Reduce the heat to very low, stir in the crème fraîche and bring to a gentle simmer. Add the cheese and the bacon and stir until the cheese has melted. The sauce should be very thick, so keep it over a low heat for a little longer, if needed.

❖ Meanwhile, preheat the grill to medium-high. Toast the bread on both sides and then place on a small baking tray.

❖ Pour the sauce onto one side of the toast.

❖ Place under the preheated grill until the sauce is bubbling and lightly browned.

Tip – You can swap smoked streaky bacon for smoked lardons instead, if you prefer.

•

Other cheeses that can be used in this recipe

Firm sheep's milk cheeses
Berkswell, Corra Linn

Firm goat's milk cheeses
Rachel

Corra Linn with Chorizo

Made by Selina Cairns and the team at Errington Cheese on Walston Breahead Farm in Carnwath, South Lanarkshire, Scotland, this traditionally made, clothbound, hard sheep's cheese is made by a similar method to traditional Cheddar. Unpasteurised milk from their own herd of Lacaune sheep is used with vegetarian rennet. The finished cheese has a Cheddar-like appearance with a smooth, creamy texture and a sweet, fruity, nutty flavour.

The creamy and buttery flavour of the cheese pairs well with the spicy meatiness of the chorizo in this delicious recipe.

Ingredients

75g uncooked chorizo sausage

1 medium slice of sourdough bread

75g Corra Linn cheese, sliced

Method

❖ Remove the skin from the chorizo sausage and crumble the meat into a small, dry frying pan. Cook the chorizo over a medium heat for about 10 minutes or until lightly browned, stirring occasionally.

❖ Meanwhile, preheat the grill to medium-high. Toast the bread on both sides and then place on a small baking tray.

❖ Spoon the chorizo over one side of the toast. Lay the cheese slices on top.

❖ Place under the preheated grill until the cheese has melted and is starting to bubble.

•

Other cheeses that can be used in this recipe

Firm sheep's milk cheeses
Berkswell, Lord of the Hundreds

Firm goat's milk cheeses
Rachel

BUFFALO'S MILK CHEESES

Buffalo's milk contains 58 per cent more calcium, 40 per cent more protein and 40 per cent less cholesterol than cow's milk. Being lower in cholesterol and higher in protein and calcium than any of the other milks used for cheesemaking in Britain, it is highly nutritious and is also a rich source of iron, phosphorus and vitamin A.

Water buffalo have been valuable animals for work, meat and dairy purposes across Asia and India for thousands of years. It cannot be confirmed how they came to Europe but is likely to have been by either Arab traders or various tribes returning from wars and travels across Asia, although it may have been as early as the Roman period when the Romans would have brought them back from their invasions to the East. What is known is that water buffalo have been established in Italy since the early medieval period and were widespread by the eleventh century.

They were first introduced to Britain in the thirteenth century by the Earl of Cornwall, brother of Henry III. It is estimated that there are nearly 200 million water buffalo in the world with 95 per cent of them being in Asia and only a few thousand in Britain, with the first commercial herds not established until 1980.

The most famous style of cheese made with buffalo milk is mozzarella, and although the original cheese is produced around Naples and the name Mozzarella di Bufala Campana is protected by law, British mozzarella is fast establishing itself as a quality cheese.

Buffalo's milk can be used to make a variety of cheese styles, including soft and creamy, hard and even blue. There are only a handful of buffalo's milk cheeses made in Britain today, but new ones are planned as people discover the nutritional benefits of buffalo's milk and cheese. There are two British examples featured on the following pages, one mozzarella and one hard cheese.

The rich creaminess of buffalo's milk cheeses pairs well with the olive oil in the bread dough used to make ciabatta. This is not a great surprise, given that the roots of both the cheese and the bread are in Italy.

Laverstoke Park Mozzarella Italian-style

This British Mozzarella is made at Laverstoke Park Farm in Overton, Hampshire, on the organic, biodynamic farm founded in 1996 by South African champion Formula 1 racing driver, Jody Scheckter. It's made using organic pasteurised milk from their own herd of 200 milking water buffalos and vegetarian rennet.

Creamy, white, smooth and delicate with a slight citrusy tang, the cheese pairs beautifully with herby, nutty pesto to give a simple but very tasty combination. The best pesto to use for this recipe is the traditional Genovese, made with basil, pine nuts, Parmigiano-Reggiano and olive oil.

Ingredients

15cm piece of ciabatta bread, cut in half lengthways

50g pesto Genovese

4 sun-dried tomatoes in oil (from a jar), lightly drained and chopped

100g Laverstoke Park Mozzarella cheese, thinly sliced

Method

❖ Preheat the oven to 180°C/160°C fan/gas 4.

❖ Toast the ciabatta halves on both sides and then place on a small baking tray, cut-sides up.

❖ Spread the pesto on the toast. Scatter the sun-dried tomatoes over, then lay the cheese slices on top.

❖ Warm through in the oven for a few minutes, then transfer under the medium-hot grill until the cheese is bubbling and light brown.

Other cheeses that can be used in this recipe

Buffalo's milk cheeses
Pendragon

Pendragon Pizza on Toast

Made by Philip Rainbow and Nicholas and Anita Robinson of the Somerset Cheese Company at Ditcheat Hill Farm in Ditcheat, Somerset. Using pasteurised buffalo's milk from local farms and vegetarian rennet, this firm, almost Cheddar-like cheese is one of the few hard buffalo's milk cheeses made in Britain. It has a melt in the mouth, buttery, creamy texture and a surprisingly strong, savoury flavour.

Due to the fat content of buffalo milk being lower than other milks, this cheese melts beautifully and therefore lends itself perfectly to this pizza-style cheese on toast recipe.

Ingredients

15cm piece of ciabatta bread, cut in half lengthways

4 teaspoons tomato purée (use the sun-dried version for a more intense flavour)

1 plum tomato, sliced

4 fresh basil leaves, torn into small pieces

100g Pendragon cheese, thinly sliced

1 teaspoon olive oil

a pinch of freshly ground black pepper

Method

❖ Preheat the oven to 180°C/160°C fan/gas 4.

❖ Toast the ciabatta halves on both sides and then place on a small baking tray, cut-sides up.

❖ Spread the tomato purée over the toast. Arrange the tomato slices on top, then scatter over the basil.

❖ Lay the cheese slices on top. Drizzle over the olive oil, then sprinkle with the black pepper.

❖ Warm through in the oven for a few minutes, then transfer under the medium-hot grill until the cheese is bubbling and light brown.

•

Other cheeses that can be used in this recipe

Buffalo's milk cheeses
Laverstoke Park Mozzarella

WELSH RAREBIT

Some sources suggest that Welsh Rabbit or Rarebit originates with a favourite foodstuff in the valleys of South Wales. The recipe called for a lump of cheese being placed into beaten eggs and milk, with onion, salt and pepper added and then baked in the oven until the cheese had melted and the mixture had set. It would have traditionally been eaten with bread and butter and vinegar.

The concept of covering toast in melted cheese with mustard has been popular in Wales since the 1500s, when it was called Caws Pobi, Welsh for toasted cheese. Andre Boorde wrote a book entitled *Fyrst Book of the Introduction of Knowledge* in 1542 and in the chapter about Wales he wrote 'I do love cawse baby, good rosted cheese'.

There is a rather unkind story in a book of jokes published in 1526 called *C Merie Talys* (100 Merry Tales) telling how God asked Saint Peter to remove all of the Welsh from heaven as they were causing too many problems. He did this by standing outside the Pearly Gates and shouting 'Caws Pobi', and as a result, all of the Welsh people ran outside the gates, such was their love of cheese. The story at the time went on to say that this was why there are no Welshmen in heaven. There is, of course, absolutely no evidence of any sort to support any part of the story.

There is also a legend that the Welsh were banned from eating rabbits caught on the estates of the nobility, and turned to cheese as a substitute, again not substantiated in any way. The term 'Welsh Rabbit' was first recorded in 1725, according to the *Oxford English Dictionary*, when it was believed that the name was a form of joke, but there are no definitive interpretations. It was common practice at the time to use fanciful names for everyday dishes, either to make them sound grander or as a form of humour. Other examples are 'Toad in the Hole', 'Bombay Duck' and 'Mock Turtle Soup', which contain neither toad, nor duck, nor turtle.

In *The Art of Cookery Made Plain and Simple*, published in 1747 by Hannah Glasse, whom many believed to be the first ever 'domestic goddess', there was a recipe for Welsh Rabbit, Scotch Rabbit and two versions of English Rabbit.

This and other eighteenth century cookbooks show it as being a popular dish enjoyed in taverns or served as a home supper dish, with not only Welsh Rabbit, but also Scotch Rabbit, Irish Rabbit and English Rabbit.

Scotch Rabbit was made by buttering the toast and topping it with grilled cheese and not adding any mustard, as in the original Welsh recipe.

Irish Rabbit used toasted soda bread as the base and stout in the cheese mix.

English Rabbit involved toasting the bread, then soaking it in red wine and allowing it to soak it up before topping with the cheese (no mustard) and finishing off under the grill.

'Welsh Rarebit' was first used as a term in 1785 in a cookbook by Francis Grose, when it is believed that 'rabbit' was corrupted to become 'rarebit' in an effort to make the dish sound grander.

Although Welsh Rarebit is the original and best known recipe, all of the other national versions have been brought up to date and there are also modern variants named 'Buck Rarebit' and 'Blushing Bunny'.

Buck Rarebit is basically Welsh Rarebit with a fried egg on top and Blushing Bunny is Welsh Rarebit blended with tomato soup.

In northern France, in the Nord-Pas-de-Calais region, there is also a version of Welsh rarebit called 'Le Welsh'.

In this section of the book, specific cheeses are not recommended, but a good-quality mature Cheddar is ideal for each recipe. Should you wish to vary the recipes, any traditional British firm cheese is suitable, including Lancashire, Cheshire, Wensleydale, Red Leicester, Double Gloucester or Caerphilly.

A thick slice of crusty, soft, white bread such as bloomer or farmhouse is the natural favourite for the creamy, sauce-like consistency of rarebit and is recommended for most of the recipes in this section – a thick slice is recommended as the bread is soft and will squash down a little during cooking. The two exceptions are Irish Rarebit, which uses soda bread, and English Rarebit, which rings the changes and uses granary bread. The simple reason for these exceptions is that the original recipes specified these traditional breads.

For the calendar- and diary-conscious amongst you, please note . . . National Welsh Rarebit Day is on 3rd September every year.

To make a Scotch rabbit.

TOAST a piece of bread very nicely on both sides, butter it, cut a slice of cheese about as big as the bread, toast it on both sides, and lay it on the bread.

To make a Welsh rabbit.

TOAST the bread on both sides, then toast the cheese on one side, lay it on the toast, and with a hot iron brown the other side. You may rub it over with mustard.

To make an English rabbit.

TOAST a piece of brown bread on both sides, then lay it in a plate before the fire, pour a glass of red wine over it, and let it soak the wine up; then cut some cheese very thin, and lay it very thick over the bread, and put it in a tin oven before the fire, and it will be toasted and browned presently. Serve it away hot.

Extract from *The Art of Cookery Made Plain and Simple*,
Hannah Glasse, 1747

Welsh Rarebit: The Original and Best

Many modern recipes for Welsh Rarebit start by making a roux of butter and flour to create a creamy sauce topping, but it is believed that the original recipe would have been far simpler. The key to it being an original Welsh Rarebit is to include beer and mustard in the topping. Although the quantity of beer used is small, it is worth using a full-flavoured dark beer such as a porter or stout. It is essential to use a good thick slice of bread, preferably a soft and crusty bloomer as the base for this recipe.

Ingredients

60g mature Cheddar cheese of your choice, grated

2 teaspoons unsalted butter, softened

1 teaspoon Worcestershire sauce

1 teaspoon English mustard

2 teaspoons of your favourite dark beer (see Tip)

1 thick slice of crusty white bloomer or farmhouse bread

Method

❖ Preheat the grill to medium-high.

❖ In a small bowl, mix the cheese, butter, Worcestershire sauce, mustard and beer together to a rough paste.

❖ Toast the bread on both sides and then place on a small baking tray.

❖ Spread the cheese mixture on one side of the toast.

❖ Place under the preheated grill until the cheesy topping is bubbling and starting to brown.

Tip – What to do with the leftover beer? Drink it, of course, and enjoy!

•

Other cheeses that can be used in this recipe

Cheddars
any of your choice

Firm cheeses
Red Leicester, Double Gloucester

Crumbly cheeses
Cheshire, Lancashire, Wensleydale

Scotch Rarebit

The original Hannah Glasse recipe instructs 'toast a piece of bread very nicely on both sides, butter it, cut a slice of cheese about as big as the bread, toast it on both sides, and lay it on the bread'. This modern adaptation is probably the simplest recipe in the book and can be made in just a few minutes. The key difference between this and other recipes is that the toast is buttered.

Ingredients

1 thick slice of crusty white bloomer or farmhouse bread

2 teaspoons unsalted butter

60g mature Cheddar cheese of your choice, thinly sliced

Method

❖ Preheat the grill to medium-high.

❖ Toast the bread on both sides and then place on a small baking tray.

❖ Butter the toast on one side, then lay the cheese slices on top.

❖ Place under the preheated grill until the cheese is bubbling and starting to brown.

•

Other cheeses that can be used in this recipe

Cheddars
any of your choice – Isle of Mull is recommended

Firm cheeses
Red Leicester, Double Gloucester

Crumbly cheeses
Cheshire, Lancashire, Wensleydale

Irish Rarebit

The key differences with Irish Rarebit are that soda bread is used as the base and Guinness is added in place of beer. This recipe also uses a wholegrain mustard for additional texture. As soda bread is made using baking powder instead of yeast as a raising agent and uses buttermilk in the dough, it results in a sweeter flavour and an almost cake-like texture.

Ingredients

60g mature Cheddar cheese of your choice, grated

2 teaspoons unsalted butter, softened

1 teaspoon plain flour

1 teaspoon wholegrain mustard

1 tablespoon Guinness

1 medium slice of soda bread

Method

❖ Preheat the grill to medium-high.

❖ Mix the cheese, butter, flour, mustard and Guinness together in a small saucepan. Heat gently, stirring continuously, until the mixture has melted and combined.

❖ Toast the bread on both sides and then place on a small baking tray.

❖ Spread the cheese mixture on one side of the toast.

❖ Place under the preheated grill until the cheesy topping is bubbling and starting to brown.

•

Other cheeses that can be used in this recipe

Cheddars
any of your choice

Firm cheeses
Red Leicester, Double Gloucester

Crumbly cheeses
Cheshire, Lancashire, Wensleydale

English Rarebit

Although Welsh Rarebit is traditionally considered to be an English dish, the original sources quoted at the start also recognise a separate English Rabbit, made by using red wine to soak into the bread. Brown bread is used in the original recipe, for which granary has been substituted here to reflect the style of brown bread made at the time, and a greater quantity of cheese is used, making this a very filling snack reflective of the indulgent eating and drinking habits of the English in the Georgian period.

Ingredients

1 medium slice of granary bread

2 tablespoons red wine

75g mature Cheddar cheese of your choice, sliced

Method

* Preheat the grill to medium-high.

* Toast the bread on both sides and then place on a plate.

* Drizzle 1 tablespoon red wine over one side of the toast. Turn the toast over and drizzle over the remaining wine. When the toast has soaked up all the wine, transfer it to a small baking tray.

* Lay the cheese slices on top, making sure the toast is fully covered.

* Place under the preheated grill until the cheese is bubbling and starting to brown.

•

Other cheeses that can be used in this recipe

This has to be made with Cheddar!

BRITISH CHEESE ON TOAST

Buck Rarebit

Buck Rarebit is simply Welsh Rarebit with a poached egg on top. It is said that poached eggs are quick and simple to make but take a lifetime to master.

A simple technique that can be used results in a perfect soft-yolk poached egg every time. Carefully crack the egg into a fine sieve (this allows the watery parts of the white to drain away – it's this watery part that goes stringy during cooking and turns the water cloudy). Gently pour the egg into a pan of simmering water, turn the heat off and leave the egg to poach for 3 minutes (for a perfect soft-yolk egg). Remove with a slotted spoon and drain.

Ingredients

60g mature Cheddar cheese of your choice, grated

2 teaspoons unsalted butter, softened

1 teaspoon Worcestershire sauce

1 teaspoon English mustard

2 teaspoons of your favourite dark beer

1 thick slice of crusty white bloomer or farmhouse bread

1 medium egg, poached (see intro)

Method

- ❖ Preheat the grill to medium-high.

- ❖ In a small bowl, mix the cheese, butter, Worcestershire sauce, mustard and beer together to a rough paste.

- ❖ Toast the bread on both sides and then place on a small baking tray.

- ❖ Spread the cheese mixture on one side of the toast.

- ❖ Place under the preheated grill until the cheesy topping is bubbling and starting to brown.

- ❖ Meanwhile, poach the egg as described in the introduction above. Place the poached egg on top of the grilled cheesy topping.

•

Other cheeses that can be used in this recipe

Cheddars
any of your choice

Firm cheeses
Red Leicester, Double Gloucester

Crumbly cheeses
Cheshire, Lancashire, Wensleydale

Other Rarebits

Welsh Rarebit has spread all over the world since Georgian times and is much loved in its many versions. In addition to the recipes on the previous pages, there are numerous recipes for various Rarebits, an eclectic selection of which (titles only) are listed below.

Leek and Caerphilly Rarebit

French Rarebit – with Brie

Lady Shaftesbury's Rarebit – with cream

Mrs Rundell's Rarebit – with egg yolks

Jamaican Rarebit – with shrimps

Oyster and Ale Rarebit

Oregon Rarebit – with Pinot Noir

Mock Crab Rarebit – with anchovies

Quebec Rarebit – with Madeira

Cider Rarebit

Sardine Rarebit

Smoked Haddock Rarebit

Tomato Cheese Rarebit

Yorkshire Rarebit – with ham and egg

Locket's Savoury Rarebit – with pear

Onion Rarebit

Acknowledgements

I really don't know where to start, as there are so many people I want to thank for helping me bring this book to you, so in no particular order, a huge thank you to . . .

First and foremost I would like to thank my wife, Amanda, who has put up with me during the researching and writing of this book, and for acting as chief taster of the recipes (except for the blue cheeses – she doesn't like them, silly woman).

My daughters, Selina, Holly and Felicity, for pretending to be interested in Dad's latest idea of writing a book.

My mum, Olive, for being my number one fan and thinking everything I do is going to be brilliant.

Ann Horsnell, not only a good friend, but also the inspiration behind the book's concept.

Before writing this book, I ran a cheese and wine shop and restaurant, where some of the recipes actually came from. I worked with an amazing team who helped me over many years' experimenting with recipes. There are too many to name here but I would particularly like to thank Lizzi Heath and Sam Badgery.

When I started in the world of cheese, I sought help from many people and the person who gave me the most encouragement, inspiration and guidance was Tim Rowcliffe, a man who has given his life to cheese.

Over the years, I have visited and spoken with many, many great cheesemakers throughout Britain, and I would like to thank them all for their tireless efforts to bring the most amazing cheeses to our plates. There are too many to mention individually but there are a few who tolerated my visits and my endless questions above and beyond the call of duty . . .

Jamie Montgomery, Mary Quicke, Mike Smales, Michaela Allam, Pete Humphries, Phil Stansfield and Debbie Mumford.

And finally, this book would not exist at all were it not for the amazingly professional team at Headline, particularly Lindsey Evans, Publisher, for having the faith and confidence to publish my first book, and Kate Miles, for being such a patient and supportive Senior Editor. Also, Anne Sheasby, Copy Editor, for being the best taskmaster and making it all come together so well. Thanks also to Antonia Whitton, Louise Rothwell and Ellie Morley.

Thank you everyone.

Recommended Cheese Shops

Having worked for many years in the cheese business, as a retailer, wholesaler, restauranteur, consultant and cheese judge, I have had the privilege and pleasure of visiting many superb cheese shops throughout Britain.

Whilst not purporting to be a comprehensive list, these are some of the shops I would highly recommend for their range of cheeses, knowledge and experience. I am sure there are many more fine cheese shops which I haven't had the pleasure of visiting, but this is my personal list arranged in alphabetical order.

The Artisan Cheesemonger
www.theartisancheesemonger.com
❖ 40–42 High Street, Holywood, County Down, Northern Ireland, BT18 9AD
028 9042 4281

The Bristol Cheesemonger
www.bristol-cheese.co.uk
❖ Unit 8, Cargo 2, Museum Street, Bristol, BS1 6ZA
0117 929 2320

Cartmel Cheeses
www.cartmelcheeses.co.uk
❖ 1 & 2 Unsworth's Yard, Cartmel, Cumbria, LA11 6PG
01539 534307

Cheese At Leadenhall
www.cheeseatleadenhall.co.uk
* 4–5 Leadenhall Market, London, EC3V 1LR
  020 7929 1697

Cheese Etc
www.cheese-etc.co.uk
* 17 Reading Road, Pangbourne, Berkshire, RG8 7LU
  0118 984 3323

The Cheese Shed
www.thecheeseshed.com
* 41 Fore Street, Bovey Tracey, Newton Abbot, Devon,
  TQ13 9AD
  01626 835599

The Cheese Society
www.thecheesesociety.co.uk
* 1 St Martin's Lane, Lincoln, LN2 1HY
  01522 511003

Cheezelo
www.cheezelo.com
* 46 Chalton Street, Euston, London, NW1 1JB
  020 7380 0099

Country Cheeses
www.countrycheeses.co.uk
* Market Road, Tavistock, Devon, PL19 0BW
  01822 615035
* 26 Fore Street, Topsham, Devon, EX3 0HD
  01392 877746
* 1 Ticklemore Street, Totnes, Devon, TQ9 5EJ
  01803 865926

The Courtyard Dairy
www.thecourtyarddairy.co.uk
* Crows Nest Barn, Austwick, Settle, North Yorkshire, LA2 8AS
  01729 823291

The Fine Cheese Company
www.finecheeseshops.co.uk
* 29–31 Walcot Street, Bath, BA1 5BN
  01225 448748
* 17 Motcomb Street, Belgravia, London, SW1 8LB
  01225 617953

George & Joseph
www.georgeandjoseph.co.uk
* 140 Harrogate Road, Chapel Allerton, Leeds, LS7 4NZ
  0113 345 0203

George Mewes
www.georgemewescheese.co.uk
* 106 Byres Road, Glasgow, G12 8TB
  0141 334 5900
* 3 Dean Park Street, Stockbridge, Edinburgh, EH4 1JN
  0131 332 5900

Hamish Johnston
www.hamishjohnston.com
* 48 Northcote Road, Battersea, London, SW11 1PA
  020 7738 0741

I.J. Mellis

www.mellischeese.net

- ❖ 30a Victoria Street, Edinburgh, EH1 2JW
  0131 226 6215
- ❖ 330 Morningside Road, Edinburgh, EH10 4QJ
  0131 447 8889
- ❖ 6 Bakers Place, Stockbridge, Edinburgh, EH3 6SY
  0131 225 6566
- ❖ 492 Great Western Road, Glasgow, G12 8EW
  0141 339 8998
- ❖ 149 South Street, St Andrews, KY16 9UN
  01334 471410

La Fromagerie

www.lafromagerie.co.uk

- ❖ 2–6 Moxon Street, Marylebone, London, W1U 4EW
  020 7935 0341
- ❖ 30 Highbury Park, London, N5 2AA
  020 7359 7440
- ❖ 52 Lamb's Conduit Street, London, WC1N 3LL
  020 7242 1044

Madame Fromage

www.madamefromage.co.uk ✓

- ❖ 21 Castle Arcade, Cardiff, CF10 1BW
  029 2064 4888

Mike's Fancy Cheese

www.mfcheese.com

- ❖ 41 Little Donegall Street, Belfast, BT1 2JD
  07794 570420

The Mousetrap Cheeseshop

www.mousetrapcheese.co.uk

* 6 Church Street, Ludlow, Herefordshire, SY8 1AP
  01584 879556
* 3 School Lane, Leominster, Herefordshire, HR6 8AA
  01568 615512
* 30 Church Street, Hereford, Herefordshire, HR1 2LR
  01432 353423

Neal's Yard Dairy

www.nealsyarddairy.co.uk

* 9 Park Street, Borough Market, London, SE1 9AB
  020 7500 7520
* Arch 8, Lucey Way, Bermondsey, London, SE16 3UF
  020 7500 7654
* 17 Shorts Gardens, Seven Dials, London, WC2H 9AT
  020 7500 7520

Paxton & Whitfield

www.paxtonandwhitfield.co.uk

* 93 Jermyn Street, St. James, London, SW1Y 6JE
  020 7321 0621
* 22 Cale Street, Chelsea, London, SW3 3QU
  020 7584 0751
* 13 Wood Street, Stratford-upon-Avon, CV37 6JF
  01789 415544
* 1 John Street, Bath, BA1 2JL
  01225 466403

Pong Cheese

www.pongcheese.co.uk
Online only

Rippon Cheese Store
www.ripponcheeselondon.com
- ❖ 26 Upper Tachbrook Street, Pimlico, London, SW1V 1SW
  020 7931 0628

Teddington Cheese
www.teddingtoncheese.co.uk
- ❖ 42 Station Road, Teddington, Middlesex, TW11 9AA
  020 8977 6868
- ❖ 74 Hill Rise, Richmond, Surrey, TW10 6UB
  020 8948 5794

Conversion Charts

Conversions are approximate and have been rounded up or down. Follow one set of measurements only – do not mix metric and imperial.

Weights

Metric	Imperial	Metric	Imperial
10 g	¼ oz	225 g	8 oz
15 g	½ oz	250 g	9 oz
20 g	¾ oz	280 g	10 oz
25 g	1 oz	300 g	10½ oz
35 g	1¼ oz	350 g	12 oz
40 g	1½ oz	375 g	13 oz
55 g	2 oz	400 g	14 oz
70 g	2½ oz	425 g	15 oz
85 g	3 oz	450 g	1 lb
100 g	3½ oz	500 g	1 lb 2 oz
115 g	4 oz	600 g	1 lb 5 oz
140 g	5 oz	750 g	1 lb 10 oz
175 g	6 oz	900 g	2 lb
200 g	7 oz	1 kg	2 lb 4 oz
		2 kg	4 lb 8 oz

Volume

Metric	Imperial	Metric	Imperial
5 ml	1 teaspoon	175 ml	6 fl oz
15 ml	1 tablespoon	200 ml	7 fl oz
30 ml	1 fl oz / 2 tablespoons	225 ml	8 fl oz
45 ml	3 tablespoons	250 ml	9 fl oz
50 ml	2 fl oz	300 ml	10 fl oz (½ pint)
60 ml	4 tablespoons	350 ml	12 fl oz
75 ml	2½ fl oz	400 ml	14 fl oz
90 ml	6 tablespoons	500 ml	18 fl oz
100 ml	3½ fl oz	600 ml	20 fl oz (1 pint)
125 ml	4 fl oz	900 ml	1½ pints
150 ml	5 fl oz (¼ pint)	1 litre	1¾ pints

Measurements

Metric	Imperial	Metric	Imperial
5 mm	¼ inch	10 cm	4 inches
1 cm	½ inch	15 cm	6 inches
2 cm	¾ inch	18 cm	7 inches
2.5 cm	1 inch	20 cm	8 inches
3 cm	1¼ inches	23 cm	9 inches
5 cm	2 inches	25 cm	10 inches
7.5 cm	3 inches	30 cm	12 inches

Index of Cheeses

C = Cow G = Goat S = Sheep B = Buffalo U/P = Unpasteurised/Pasteurised

Th = Thermised V = Vegetarian T = Traditional O = Organic

Name of Cheese	Cheesemaker					Page
Appleby's Cheshire	Appleby's	C	U	V		109
Appleby's Double Gloucester	Appleby's	C	U	V		87
Barkham Blue	Two Hoots Cheese	C	P	V		247
Baron Bigod	Fen Farm Dairy	C	U	T		53
Bath Soft	Bath Soft Cheese Co	C	P	T	O	51
Beauvale	Cropwell Bishop Creamery	C	P	T		237
Belton Farm White Cheshire	Belton Farm	C	P	V		115
Berkswell	Berkswell Cheese	S	U	T		285
Bix	Nettlebed Creamery	C	P	T	O	67
Blue Murder	Highland Fine Cheeses	C	P	V		239
Cerney Ash	Cerney Cheese	G	U	V		263
Colston Bassett Stilton	Colston Bassett Dairy	C	P	V/T		225
Cornish Blue	Cornish Cheese Co	C	U	V		245
Cornish Yarg	Lynher Dairies Cheese Co	C	P	V		137
Corra Linn	Errington Cheese	S	U	V		291
Cote Hill Blue	Cote Hill Cheese	C	U	V		251
Cropwell Bishop Stilton	Cropwell Bishop Creamery	C	P	V		227

Name of Cheese	Cheesemaker					Page
Keen's Cheddar	Keen's Cheddar	C	U	T		32
Kilcreen	Dart Mountain Cheese	C	P	T		163
Kit Calvert Wensleydale	Wensleydale Dairy Products	C	P	T		127
Laverstoke Park Buffalo Mozzarella	Laverstoke Park Farm	B	P	V	O	297
Lincolnshire Poacher	Lincolnshire Poacher Cheese	C	U	T		42
Lord of the Hundreds	Traditional Cheese Dairy Co	S	U	V		289
Lyburn Garlic and Nettle	Lyburn Farmhouse Cheesemakers	C	P	V		193
Maida Vale	Village Maid Cheese	C	Th	V		173
Martell's Double Gloucester	Charles Martell & Son	C	U/P	V		85
Mayfield	Alsop and Walker	C	P	V		159
Medita	Sussex High Weald Dairy	C	P	V	O	214
Montgomery's Cheddar	J.A & E. Montgomery	C	U	T		28
Montgomery's Smoked Cheddar	J.A & E. Montgomery	C	U	T		183
Morn Dew	White Lake Cheese	C	P	V		161
Mouth Almighty	Saddleworth Cheese Co	C	P	V		103
Mrs Bourne's Mature Cheshire	H.S. Bourne	C	P	V		111
Mrs Kirkham's Lancashire	Mrs Kirkham's Lancashire Cheese	C	U	T		97
Muldoon's Picnic	Saddleworth Cheese Co	C	P	V		101
Norbury Blue	Norbury Park Farm Cheese Co	C	U	V		249

Name of Cheese	Cheesemaker				Page
Ogleshield	J.A & E. Montgomery	C	P	T	157
Old Winchester	Lyburn Farmhouse Cheesemakers	C	P	V	145
Pendragon	Somerset Cheese Co	B	P	V	299
Penyston Brie	Daylesford Organic	C	U	V	O	61
Perl Wen	Caws Cenarth Cheese	C	P	V	O	55
Pitchfork Cheddar	Trethowan's Dairy	C	U	T	O	34
Quicke's Cheddar	Quicke's Traditional	C	P	T	36
Quicke's Elderflower	Quicke's Traditional	C	P	T	201
Quicke's Oak Smoked Cheddar	Quicke's Traditional	C	P	V	181
Rachel	White Lake Cheese	G	Th	V	265
Ragstone	Neal's Yard Creamery	G	P	T	259
Real Yorkshire Wensleydale	Wensleydale Dairy Products	C	P	T	123
Red Fox	Belton Farm	C	P	V	79
Renegade Monk	Feltham's Farm	C	P	V	243
Richard III Wensleydale	Fortmayne Farm Dairy	C	P	V	121
Riseley	Village Maid Cheese	S	Th	V	279
Rollright	King Stone Dairy	C	P	T	171
Rosary	Rosary Goats Cheese	G	P	V	261
Sharpham	Sharpham Partnership	C	U	V	63
Sharpham Chive and Garlic	Sharpham Partnership	C	U	V	197
Sinodun Hill	Norton and Yarrow Cheese	G	U	V	269
Smart's Double Gloucester	Smart's Traditional Gloucester	C	U	V	89

Name of Cheese	Cheesemaker					Page
Sparkenhoe Red Leicester	Leicestershire Handmade Cheese	C	U	T		73
St James	St James Cheese	S	U	T		287
Stichelton	Stichelton Dairy	C	U	T		229
Stinking Bishop	Charles Martell & Son	C	P	V		169
Sussex Charmer	Bookham Harrison Farms	C	P	V		147
Sussex Slipcote	Sussex High Weald Dairy	S	P	V		283
Teifi	Caws Teifi Cheese	C	U	V	O	151
Ticklemore	Sharpham Partnership	G	P	V		267
Tornegus	Eastside Cheese Co	C	P	V		203
Triple Rose	Ballylisk of Armagh	C	P	V		65
Truffler	Ford Farm Cheesemakers	C	P	V		207
Tunworth	Hampshire Cheeses	C	P	T		57
Waterloo	Village Maid Cheese	C	Th	V		49
Westcombe Cheddar	Westcombe Dairy	C	U	T		30
Westcombe Smoked Cheddar	Westcombe Dairy	C	U	T		187
White Nancy	White Lake Cheese	G	Th	V		271
Wigmore	Village Maid Cheese	S	Th	V		277
Wild Garlic Yarg	Lynher Dairies Cheese Co	C	P	V		195
Yorkshire Fettle	Shepherds Purse Cheeses	C	P	V		212
Young Buck	Mike's Fancy Cheese	C	U	T		241

Index of Recipes

BRITISH CHEESE ON TOAST

General Index